gospeL
MEDITATIONS
on the
PSALMS

"*Gospel Meditations on the Psalms* provides a healthy blend of biblical accuracy, relatable application, and gospel focus. Each of the psalm summaries will enrich deeper learning and encourage devotional living. The reader will discover the powerful simplicity of letting the gospel do its work. The devotional summaries challenged me to consider, apply, and live out the gospel principles they so poignantly explained!"

—**Kurt Skelly**, senior pastor of Faith Baptist Church, Fredericksburg, Virginia, and frequent speaker in churches, colleges, and conferences around the world

"In this devotional, Chris Anderson, Abby Huffstutler, and Joe Tyrpak function as tour guides to the Psalms. They orient us to the world of the Psalms, they share with us some of their special sites, and they inspire us to travel more extensively in this sublime portion of God's Word. Reading through these meditations will bless your soul and will encourage you to return often to the Psalms for spiritual nourishment."

—**Dan Estes**, PhD, former pastor of Linwood Baptist Church, Worthington, Ohio, Distinguished Professor of Old Testament at Cedarville University, and author of *Handbook on the Wisdom Books and Psalms*

"The Psalms are a mirror of the human heart. They run the gamut from doubt, fear, and anger to love, joy, and hope. But they not only reveal our emotional ups and downs—they also reveal the heart of God to us in Jesus. In these *Gospel Meditations on the Psalms*, the authors faithfully unpack the text and point us to Christ as our hope and joy. Grab your Bible, and be prepared for some nourishing spiritual food."

—**Rhett Dodson**, PhD, pastor of Grace Presbyterian Church, Hudson, Ohio, and author of *Marching to Zion: Ancient Psalms for Modern Pilgrims*

"How can I find the gospel in the Psalms? Too often, we reduce the gospel to refer only to the part that saves us. But the gospel is the whole of Jesus' life and ministry, and so, understood in that sense, the Psalms are a great place to find meditations on the gospel. Joe, Abby, and Chris have done an excellent job bathing our thoughts in the blessed waters of the Psalms. Each devotional is another scrub on our hearts with the brush of God's grace, mercy, and peace from God the Father and our Lord Jesus Christ."

—**Matt Walker**, pastor of College Park Baptist Church, Cary, North Carolina

© 2023 by Church Works Media. All rights reserved.

Unless otherwise indicated, Scripture quotations are from the ESV Bible (*The Holy Bible, English Standard Version*), copyright © 2001 by Crossway, a publishing ministry of Good News Publishers. Used by permission. All rights reserved.

Thank you to Hanna Buckland Photography for the lovely cover photo, taken in Inverness, Scotland. Used by permission.

The articles on Day 1 and Day 31 are edited excerpts from Chris Anderson, *Theology That Sticks: The Life-Changing Power of Exceptional Hymns* (Church Works Media, 2022).

Introduction

The Psalms are balms. They have brought help and healing to God's people for over 3,000 years. Scripture's 150 inspired songs give us words to pray during times of joy and sorrow, triumph and loss, worship and conviction. They are so vibrant, so beautiful, so real.

For these and many other reasons, we're excited to make *Gospel Meditations on the Psalms* the most recent addition to this devotional series. As always, we have labored to be expositional. We're not just commenting on small portions of select psalms, but on entire psalms. So let me urge readers to start with Scripture as you dive into each meditation—read the psalm first, then look back at it as you read our explanations. We've included verse numbers throughout the articles to help you see why we're saying what we are about these God-breathed poems. We feel the responsibility to "prove it" with the sacred text rather than just waxing eloquent about our own ideas. So we invite you to be Bereans (Acts 17:11): compare what we've written with the psalms themselves to be sure we're not making stuff up.

We hope that you'll also find the devotionals to be practical. What the psalm-writers have given us is life-changing, and so we aim to make real-life applications. Don't just read the psalms; *pray* them, *obey* them, and as you're able, *sing* them.

Finally, we have endeavored to make these meditations distinctly Christian. We don't believe that every single psalm contains an overt reference to Jesus Christ. However, we write with the conviction that God the Spirit carried along every author of Scripture in order to magnify God the Son. We write with the conviction that "the Scriptures point to" Jesus (John 5:39 NLT). So we've taken up the challenge of Isaac Watts to "Christianize" the psalms, as his introduction to his eighteenth-century psalter explains: "In all places I have kept my grand design in view; and that is to teach [the psalmist] to speak like a Christian." With Luke 24:44–45 as our guide—and with a healthy respect for authorial intent—we have labored to show that the psalms propel us to Jesus, and we have therefore made gospel applications over and over again. We don't need just truth, or compassion, or songs—we need *Jesus*!

Joe and I are grateful to include Abby Huffstutler as a first-time author with Church Works Media. Abby's fingerprints are all over the previous devotionals in the *Gospel Meditations* series and our other books; she's our go-to copyeditor. But this time she's stepping *in front* of the curtain, writing her own articles as well as editing Joe's and mine. As a fellow word nerd and as a mature sister in Christ, her contributions to this volume are profound.

May the Lord use this little book to comfort the hurting, settle the confused, and encourage all of the redeemed to find their hope and delight in God alone. Grace!

Chris Anderson

DAY **1**

A Primer on the Psalms
READ PSALM 103
"Singing psalms and hymns and spiritual songs" COLOSSIANS 3:16

Part of the power of the book of Psalms is its raw honesty. It's filled with excruciating pain and confusion, but also with exuberant joy and celebration. Reformer John Calvin calls the psalms "an anatomy of all the parts of the soul." He writes, "The Holy Spirit has here drawn to the life all the griefs, sorrows, fears, doubts, hopes, cares, perplexities, in short, all the distracting emotions, with which the minds of men are want to be agitated." The psalms teach us how to think and feel.

How to Think and Feel about God: The Psalms of Exaltation—The psalms point us to God, and they tell us to delight in Him. They are teeming with the names of God (nouns), the attributes of God (adjectives), and the works of God (verbs). They remind us that God is *ours*—our Creator, our Shepherd, and so on. They call us to give Him "glorious praise" (Psalm 66:2). The unmistakable focus of the psalms is God.

How to Think and Feel about Sin: The Psalms of Repentance—The psalms of confession are well-worn in my Bibles. They have taught me how to respond to my own sinful failures. First John 1:9 invites us to "confess our sins," but Psalms 32 and 51 model *how*. Commentators generally list seven "penitential psalms": Psalms 6, 32, 38, 51, 102, 130, and 143. They reveal not only the sorrow of sin unconfessed, but the relief and joy of sin forgiven (32:1). Learning to pray these psalms back to God will be a boon for your soul, especially when you fail. Again.

How to Think and Feel about Injustice: The Psalms of Imprecation—The psalms encourage us to be angry in the face of evil and teach us to pray for God to bring justice to the wicked. While many Christians feel uncomfortable about the imprecatory psalms, or even ashamed of them as though they are unworthy of God, they are part of the inspired Scriptures. Yes, you should pause before praying for God to judge the wicked, recognizing your own sinfulness and God's mercy to you. And you should pray for sinners to come to faith in Christ. But praying for justice is good, even godly. Revenge, God says, is not an option (James 1:19–20). But if the psalms' prayers for justice make you uncomfortable, ask yourself why.

How to Think and Feel about Sorrow and Confusion: The Psalms of Lament—The modern church doesn't lament well, despite the fact that sixty of the psalms—*a staggering forty percent*—are expressions of sorrow! Undeterred by the sheer numbers, we essentially edit the sad songs out of the Scriptures and out of our church services. People come to church with broken hearts and are confronted with slaphappy songs. Christians who are opposed to the prosperity gospel in theory are still uncomfortable with the psalms which express sorrow, confusion, and even anger. But God's provision of sad songs is a mercy to people living in a broken world. They show us that we're not crazy, that life really does hurt, and that God doesn't expect us to pretend we're okay when we're grieving. I often challenge people to *pray mad*—but to keep praying to the God Who has revealed Himself as our Refuge and Shield. The psalms of lament show us how.

The psalms have been a salve to God's people for three millennia. Our Savior sang them (Matthew 26:30) and quoted them, even from the cross (Matthew 27:46). Indeed, Jesus taught that the psalms ultimately point to Him (Luke 24:44). The church is commanded to sing them (Colossians 3:16 and Ephesians 5:19). They teach us how to sing, pray, think, and feel. Use them well!

Let the gospel drive you into the book of Psalms for your own good and for God's glory.
—CHRIS

The Secret to Happiness
READ PSALM 1

"In all that he does, he prospers." PSALM 1:3

DAY 2

The book of Psalms begins in a surprising way. First, it sounds a lot like a proverb. Psalm 1 contains life lessons, not jubilant praise. Second, it's a call to *happiness*. Maybe that surprises only me, but I've heard plenty of sermons telling me that God wants me to be holy, not happy. And Psalm 1 says that's just not true.

The first word of the Psalter is "blessed." It describes one who is not only fortunate, but *happy* (like the beatitudes in Matthew 5:3–12). Christianity isn't a life of morose misery. God wants you to have joy that is "full" as you share in Jesus' own joy (John 15:11; 16:24; 17:13). You may need to change your view of both Christianity and God. He is a generous and benevolent Giver of gladness! He wants you to be happy, and He tells you *how* through a series of three contrasts that will change your life.

Two Paths (Psalm 1:1–2)—The psalmist first contrasts two paths. It's unclear if they diverge in a yellow wood, but they do indeed diverge. The blessed person avoids the way of the *world* (v. 1)—our culture and its ungodly values—and chooses the way of the *Word* (v. 2). Notice the regression in verse 1: the person begins by walking by the wicked, soon is standing and listening to the wicked, and eventually ends up sitting down to join the wicked. The world promises freedom! Pleasure! The good life! But, as we will see, it delivers the opposite. Thankfully, there's another path—the way of the Word. The happy person lives according to the Bible. In fact, he *delights* in it, musing on it day and night. (More happiness!) So, will you base your life on the opinions of culture or the truths of Scripture?

Two Plants (Psalm 1:3–4)—Verses 3 and 4 reveal the consequences of the choice made in verses 1 and 2. The person who lives according to the Word is illustrated by a lush and healthy tree (v. 3). (Don't you love the symbolism of the psalms?!) Few things give me more enjoyment than a beautiful tree—a towering pine, a tropical palm, or a stretching live oak. But what does the imagery *mean*? That's easy. If you live according to Scripture, your life will be good: well-watered, fruitful, and fulfilling. Who doesn't want that?! On the other hand (here's the contrast), if you live according to the world, you should expect sorrow and regret. The life of the ungodly person is dry and dead—like "chaff," the dusty husks that fall to the ground when someone is winnowing wheat (v. 4). We moderns might say that the wicked person is like a tumbleweed, a hay bale, or a dry brown lawn. Who wants a life like that?

Two Destinies (Psalm 1:5–6)—Although Psalm 1 begins with an offer of happiness, its ending is deadly serious. Remember how walking with the wicked leads to a dry, sorrowful life? What could be worse? One thing: a dry and sorrowful *eternity*. Verses 5 and 6 look beyond our life on earth to our coming judgment, and they tell us that sinners will "perish"—a description of eternal damnation. We need another option. Thankfully, God gives us a final contrast. The person who lives according to the Word (v. 2) will enjoy a fruitful life (v. 3) which will culminate in *eternal* happiness (vv. 5–6).

To be clear, the way of salvation isn't reached by a series of good choices. Rather, a happy life and a happy eternity can only be received, not earned (Ephesians 2:8–9). You don't just need a fresh start; you need *Jesus*—the ultimate "Blessed Man" Who delighted in and obeyed God's Word as Psalm 1 requires. He alone can bring you peace with God, the forgiveness of your sins, and help through life's inevitable hardships. And He will one day take you to be with Himself forever. Trusting Him with your life and eternity is the only sane choice. Right?

Let the gospel warn you away from the way of the world and show you the happiness that can only come through Jesus Christ.—CHRIS

DAY 3

God Isn't Worried

READ PSALM 2

"He who sits in the heavens laughs; the Lord holds them in derision." PSALM 2:4

The second psalm is a militant anthem that asserts the supreme authority of Israel's king over every other king on earth. The Israelite nation likely sang it at coronation celebrations. In the song, God the Father and His Son, the anointed King from David's line, confront world rulers with their need to submit themselves under the authority of God and His chosen Ruler. Although the song is harsh—singing about angry rebellion, scornful laughter, and pottery-smashing wrath—every child of God should find its message mightily comforting. Consider three particularly encouraging realities.

God remains unworried about all the political mess in the world. Nations have raged against God all through history, and this posture continues in our day through unjust military aggression, the ubiquitous persecution of Christians, and the universal assault on God's design of sexuality and gender. Whenever you read this anthem, you must remind yourself that God does not respond to opposition like you probably do. He doesn't get worried. He actually finds it funny—as funny as a prison guard who watches a convict shake the bars of his cell for days on end thinking that he'll eventually break himself free. Isn't it comforting to know that there is no chance that anyone will ever overthrow God's sovereign plan for the world?

Jesus will most certainly reign as King of kings. Though this song may have been sung on many coronation days throughout Israel's history, its words could only apply in all their fullness to Jesus. Every other king in David's line was only a faint preview of Jesus. Consider verse 9, where we learn that God's chosen King will "break [the nations] with a rod of iron." Even though some of Israel's kings won military victories over other nations, only the "King of kings and Lord of lords" has been appointed by God to "rule [the nations] with a rod of iron," and He will when He returns in glory (Revelation 19:15–16). Further, consider verse 7, where God the Father anoints His chosen Ruler with the words, "You are my Son!" A thousand years after the psalm was penned, God the Father Himself audibly repeated this declaration when Jesus was baptized (Matthew 3:17) and when Jesus was transfigured (Matthew 17:5; 2 Peter 1:12–21). And God the Father definitively "declared [Jesus] to be the Son of God" when He raised Him from the dead (Romans 1:4). The first generation of Christians rightly understood that Psalm 2 referred ultimately to Jesus. Jesus is God the Son and is chosen by God the Father to rule forever as earth's Sovereign. This firm conviction filled the early church with boldness amid opposition (Acts 4:25–31; Hebrews 1:5).

There is a way for those who deserve God's wrath to enjoy His blessing. According to the final statement of the song, anyone who is raging against God's authority (and according to Romans 1–3, that's everyone) can find *blessing* rather than judgment if he or she will submit to God's chosen King. That's because Jesus the Messiah was crucified, bearing God's just punishment for all who would "take refuge in him" (v. 12). What a glorious consolation that earth's eternal Sovereign is full of humble, self-sacrificial love! Marvel that the One Who will pour out God's wrath on the world took God's wrath on Himself for all who turn to Him!

Many people liken the first two psalms in the Bible's hymnbook to a border crossing into God's kingdom. Rather than living the way of the world (Psalm 1) and rebelling against God's Son (Psalm 2), those who want to be citizens of God's kingdom must submit to Christ. They must "kiss the Son" (Psalm 2) and be united with the truly "blessed" Man (Psalm 1).

Let the gospel save you from your raging rebellion and comfort you in this tumultuous world. —JOE

Humanity's Humility & Honor

DAY 4

READ PSALM 8 & HEBREWS 2:5–8

"You have put all things under his feet." PSALM 8:6

The first and last verses of Psalm 8 are remarkably singable. As a teen, I sang at least three versions, and I can still belt out every word of those songs years later. But my appreciation of Psalm 8 has grown immensely in recent years. It's more than a psalm about how the stars point to our Creator's greatness. It's also a key theological piece that traces Scripture's creation-fall-redemption theme from Genesis 1 to Revelation 22, with important stops in the middle. Let's learn how.

Creation shows God's infinite majesty. There is a beautiful simplicity to Psalm 8. I picture David stretched out on his back in a pasture, gazing up at the night stars and marveling at their Maker. As in Psalm 19, David sees and hears in the natural world an echo of God's glory and greatness. If the heavens are high, God's glory is even higher (v. 1b). God's greatness is demonstrated by all of creation—from vast stars to "babies and infants" (v. 2). Indeed, Jesus quoted Psalm 8:2 as He received praise from children in the temple after the triumphal entry (Matthew 21:16—where, among other things, Jesus claims to be Psalm 8's Jehovah!).

Creation has been entrusted to humanity through the Dominion Mandate. Verses 3 through 8 move from the glory of God's creation to the mystery of God's relationship with humanity. David, feeling infinitely small compared to the heavens, marvels that God is mindful of humanity (vv. 3–4). We are small, yet beloved. Yes, we lack some powers that angels possess (v. 5; Hebrews 2:7). But we also have privileges angels will never experience. Our unique position is a testimony to the dignity of humanity over the rest of God's creatures: we alone bear our Maker's image. And as a testimony to God's condescending grace, He thinks of us!

But there's more here. Much more. God has actually entrusted to humanity the rest of His creation (vv. 5–8). Psalm 8 takes us way back to the Dominion Mandate of Genesis 1–2 where God deputized us as His coregents (Genesis 1:26–29; 2:15). He put into our care everything else He made—a life-changing truth that elevates the work of farmers, chemists, builders, and poets. The Dominion Mandate ennobles our everyday work. It also means that Christians must continue to steward God's world—a balanced and reasonable approach to ecology matters!

But there's still more. Sadly, God's putting the natural world into our hands in Genesis 1 and 2 is followed immediately by our abject failure in Genesis 3. We broke God's perfect world. Because of our sin, all creation groans beneath the curse. In some ways, the world is out of control—subject to war, famine, and disease—not "under our feet" as God intended (v. 6). Nevertheless, in more of God's astounding mercy, He revealed His eternal plan to clean up our mess with the Bible's first gospel promise—a Savior Who would come to reverse the curse (Genesis 3:15).

Creation will eventually come under the dominion of the perfect Man, the Lord Jesus. Psalm 8 doesn't mention Jesus by name. Ah, but He's there, and the New Testament makes the connection explicitly! Jesus is the Second Adam (Romans 5:12–21). Where the first Adam failed, Jesus triumphs. He not only saves sinners—He will save *all of creation*! Just as He fulfilled other laws in our stead, Jesus will fulfill the Dominion Mandate in our place. One day, He will make all of His creation new (Revelation 21–22) and rule with all things under *His* feet (1 Corinthians 15:27; Ephesians 1:22; Hebrews 2:6–8). God—the Creator and Re-Creator—is majestic indeed!

Let the gospel inform your understanding of the world that was, that is, and that will be.
—CHRIS

DAY 5
Chariots, Hills, and True Help
READ PSALMS 20 & 121

"Some trust in chariots and some in horses, but we trust in the name of the Lord our God."
PSALM 20:7

"It is the *object* of faith that determines the *value* of faith." This invaluable lesson was taught to me by my friend and mentor Michael Barrett. It's especially important to grasp this truth in a culture which disdains Scripture but which nods approvingly when people share a quasi-spiritual determination to "keep the faith." George Michael, a 1980s singer who was anything but an example of religious virtue, crooned, "I gotta have faith." Yes, but *in what*? Even well-meaning wishes for those fighting for their lives betray our clouded thinking: "Thoughts and prayers to so-and-so." Umm, *to* her or *for* her? Only faith in God helps. That's the point of both Psalms 20 and 121.

Faith-Building Truth from Psalm 20—Psalm 20 is a royal psalm, a prayer for God's blessing on King David. In one sense, it's unique to Israel's situation in history. But, in light of passages like 1 Timothy 2:1–4, Psalm 20 is a model prayer to pray for our political leaders. The requests are fairly general: May the Lord answer the king (or president, or prime minister) in the day of trouble, protect him, help him, support him, grant him success, and so on. What's more striking than the requests, however, is that the source of help is God and no other: "May the Lord . . . May the name of the God of Jacob . . . May he . . . May he . . . May he . . . May the Lord . . ." (vv. 1–5).

There's one more request you can sing with your best British accent, if you'd like: May God "save the king (or queen)!" (v. 9). Even the most powerful need divine aid, as verses 6–8 make unmistakably clear. Those who trust in the one true God will be blessed (vv. 6, 8b). Those who trust in "chariots" and "horses" (v. 7) will "collapse and fall" (v. 8a). Why chariots? Because chariots were the height of military strength in the Old Testament—the Sherman tanks of the ancient world, the very best that human ingenuity could muster. They weren't sinful. But as the *objects of faith*, they were vain. After all, horses and chariots wound up at the bottom of the Red Sea (Exodus 15:4).

Psalm 20:7—along with Isaiah 31:1 and Psalm 60:11—reminds us that any help besides God's is vain. In our day we might say "some trust in technology" or "education" or "hard work" or "a solid 401(k)" or "a political party" or anything else we're tempted to rely on. But the only *true* help, both for the king and for you and me, comes from the Lord. Only Jesus can meet our great salvation need and every other need we face.

Faith-Building Truth from Psalm 121—Unlike Psalm 20, Psalm 121 wasn't intended for kings. It's for the rest of us, for normal people. It's one of the "Psalms of Ascent," used when Israelites would journey from their homes to Jerusalem several times a year to worship. It's essentially a prayer for safety—for "travel mercies," as we say.

But beyond a prayer for safe arrival, it's a model prayer of dependence on God as our only true Helper (Hebrews 13:6). The genius of the psalm is in verses 1 and 2; the rest is details. The key question is, "Where does my help come from?" The psalmist had his eyes on the hills (v. 1)—perhaps in weariness from the journey, or in fear of danger from bandits. From where could David expect help? True help comes only from the Lord, the One Who made heaven and earth . . . and the hills, for that matter. It is God—our ever-attentive, never-slumbering Lord—Who keeps our feet from slipping (vv. 3–4). It is the Lord Who keeps us from growing weary and provides shade in our distress (vv. 5–6). It is the Lord Who keeps us from evil and Who preserves our lives (v. 7). Best of all, with an eye on the cross of Christ and a nod to John Newton, it is the Lord and His grace that "will lead us safely home"—not just during our lives, but in eternity (v. 8). We have no other helper. And we *need* no other helper!

Let the gospel remind you that there is no true help apart from the Lord.—CHRIS

"Why Have You Forsaken Me?"

DAY 6

READ PSALM 22

"They have pierced my hands and feet." PSALM 22:16

Following His resurrection, Jesus taught His disciples that the Old Testament Scriptures, including the Psalms, all point to Him (Luke 24:27, 44). That's not to say that every psalm has an explicit Jesus reference to spot, like an inspired "Where's Waldo?" book. Much of the Old Testament points to Jesus in a general way: the need for a perfect Prophet, Priest, and King; the temporary sacrificial system; the increasingly specific prophecies of the Messiah; and so on. But some passages are overtly Messianic, predicting Christ with unmistakable clarity. Psalm 22 is one of those. It speaks first of David, but it speaks even more emphatically of Christ.

The Sufferings of David—David, inspired by the Holy Spirit, wrote Psalm 22 to lament his own trials. He models an innocent believer being oppressed by the wicked. Here's a quick synopsis of his complaints. (Notice the back-and-forth movement between frustration and faith as he argues with himself.) He felt forsaken by God (vv. 1–2) . . . but he knew that God had shown Himself trustworthy in the past (vv. 3–5). He was discouraged by the mockery of unbelievers (vv. 6–8) . . . but he knew that God had cared for him from the womb (vv. 9–11). He was surrounded and hounded by oppressors (vv. 12–18) . . . but it caused him to plead with God for deliverance (vv. 19–21). In the end—after all his points and counterpoints—David was certain of eventual victory and vindication (vv. 22–31). Yes, David describes his troubles with a degree of hyperbole, and for a good reason: He was writing one of the Old Testament's most vivid (non-hyperbolic) predictions of Christ!

The Sufferings of Christ—Psalm 22's fuller (and obvious) intention is to point us beyond David to Jesus—the *ultimate* innocent-yet-suffering One. Like Isaiah 53, Psalm 22 reads like an eyewitness account of the crucifixion. And it's not our imagination; the New Testament repeatedly applies Psalm 22 to Jesus' life and death.

Psalm 22 predicts Jesus' incarnation. Hebrews 2:12 cites Psalm 22:22 to show that Jesus shares the humanity of His followers, calling us "brothers." Both Jesus' humanity and deity are essential to our salvation. This nod to the incarnation makes the baby descriptions of verses 9–10 all the more meaningful. In Jesus Christ, God became a man.

Psalm 22 predicts Jesus' crucifixion. It describes Jesus' *humiliation* as His garments were gambled for (Matthew 27:35; Psalm 22:18) and as He was mocked (Matthew 27:39, 43; Psalm 22:7, 8). The psalm also describes *Jesus' physical torture*—He was poured out like water; His bones were laid bare and out of joint; His heart melted like wax; His strength dried up; His hands and feet were pierced (vv. 14–16). Most importantly, the psalm describes *Jesus' spiritual agony.* Jesus endured the abandonment of His disciples silently. But He cried out in anguish when the Father turned His back on Him (Matthew 27:46; Psalm 22:1). Why this breach in Their fellowship? Why this abandonment? Because Jesus was made to be sin for us (2 Corinthians 5:21). He was exiled from the Father, separated from God by our sin (Isaiah 59:2) so that we might be forgiven and welcomed into the Father's presence. In some mysterious way, the cross shows us the Father forsaking His beloved Son for a time—"God estranged from God."

Psalm 22 predicts Jesus' vindication. David's rejoicing in verses 22–31 has a much deeper meaning in light of Jesus' resurrection and reign. Christ has won! He has triumphed over death. He is gathering "the ends of the earth" (v. 27) into His church. In the words of 1 Peter 1:10–11, Psalm 22 tells not only of "the sufferings of Christ" but also of "the subsequent glories." What a Savior!

Let the gospel cause you to marvel at Jesus' suffering on your behalf.—CHRIS

DAY 7
"I Shall Not Want"
READ PSALM 23

"Even though I walk through the valley of the shadow of death, I will fear no evil, for you are with me." PSALM 23:4

Have particular Bible passages ever become especially real to you? In January 2009, my husband presented a New Year's focus to our church: He read Psalm 23 and challenged us to make sure the Lord was our personal Shepherd. I'd known this very familiar psalm since childhood, but that year I latched onto it. I didn't know the next few years would bring multiple moves, big vocational questions, and financial hardship. But during those difficult times, I also saw concrete evidence that God is my Shepherd—an image of God woven throughout the Bible (Genesis 48:15; Psalm 28:9; Isaiah 40:11; Hebrews 13:20; Revelation 7:17). I held that psalm close and still turn to it often. What are the precious truths of Psalm 23 that comfort us in life and in death?

God's Providential Care—The psalm starts with two important words: "The LORD." This is Jehovah. The Self-existent One. And as immeasurably great as He is, He's also my personal Caregiver—*my Shepherd* (v. 1)! This metaphor is perfect. Shepherding requires a kind, gentle person—that's Jesus, the good Shepherd Who laid down His life to save His sheep (John 10). And shepherding is necessary because sheep are notoriously foolish wanderers—that's us, going our own sinful way (Isaiah 53). David takes us to a farm scene with a small stream and green grass (v. 2). There, God does what shepherds do: He gently leads us to what's good for us (v. 3). He gives us peaceful rest (v. 2) and refreshment (v. 5). And He restores us to the "paths of righteousness" (v. 3) after we've strayed. It's the pastoral setting of Jesus' Luke 15 story—where a shepherd with one hundred animals persists in rescuing *just one* who is perilously lost. The image of Jesus seeking and saving His sheep is the good news of the gospel (Luke 19:10)!

God's Constant Presence—God is with His sheep 24/7. His omnipresence is something we can hardly grasp—because we can't see Him. But this psalm tells us God is *right there* with us. When the wickedness of our world makes us afraid, God assures us that He is there and that we don't have to fear evil (v. 4). When you are near death yourself or in death's shadow as a loved one passes—God is walking in that valley with you, comforting you (v. 4). There are eight billion people on this earth, but we can still feel very lonely at times. And when we do, there is nothing like the comfort of our Shepherd beside us. Rejoice that He will never leave you.

God's Overflowing Blessing—The good Shepherd blesses His sheep until their cups are completely full—and then pours more goodness on top. Regularly, He goes beyond expectations and does good things for us—"far more abundantly than all that we ask or think" (Ephesians 3:20). Start counting your blessings, "naming them one by one" (hymn credit: Johnson Oatman). And when you've cataloged even just a little bit of what He has done for you, you'll be amazed! Then, add in the *time* factor: God's shepherding of His children is *lifelong* and then *eternal*. His "goodness and mercy" toward us will continue as long as we are alive (v. 6). And if Jesus hasn't already returned, once we die, we'll experience the blessings of living with Him in heaven forever!

This is not just a psalm for funerals. It is a place for us to run whenever we experience need. "I shall not want" (v. 1) does not mean I will never have needs. It means I will never lack His shepherding care. If I have Jesus as my Savior from sin and death, I don't need anything or anyone else. This world offers temporary comfort in a million things, like food, friends, money, vacations, drink—but none of it satisfies like Jesus does (John 4). The reality of Psalm 23 is that God is the only true Shepherd. Our safe place is with Him.

Let the gospel comfort you with the knowledge that your Shepherd will never leave you, in this life or the next.—ABBY

The Voice of the Lord

DAY 8

READ PSALM 29

"The voice of the Lord is powerful; the voice of the Lord is full of majesty." PSALM 29:4

Picture this: From above an enormous sea of water, a voice suddenly speaks, carrying wide and far and filling the space. Its magnificence is thunderous. A storm begins to churn, punctuated by loud, echoing booms of Someone speaking. Forests border this sea, and the earth begins palpably shaking. Trees are broken. Lightning flashes add to the visual and audible power, setting nature aflame. And the voice is controlling it all. *This is the Sovereign Lord*—talking, authoritatively (vv. 3–9).

Psalm 29 zeroes in on one specific aspect of God: *His voice*. The drama going on in this psalm is grand—pure, unmatched power. David doesn't let us miss it, using seven repetitions of the phrase "the voice of the Lord" to make sure we get the point: "God's voice is incredibly strong!"

As a reader, I'm captivated when an author artfully wields the tool of analogy. So, I have great respect for David's use of comparison to help us "see" God's vocal capability. Psalm 29 builds a visual description of something inherently auditory in nature—a voice—so that we can know God more fully. And here's what we're to learn: *There is a voice more powerful than all—the voice of God*. For another analogy, think about the energy and power of human voices in our world. A professor shares knowledge with such clarity and insight that students are inspired. A sports announcer describes a play-by-play, even over radio, with such emotion and detail that we feel we're there. Or a parent connects so deeply with a child, just via words, that the little one starts to understand and know love. Words are powerful. But none of these "power voices" in our experience come anywhere close to producing the scene we started with—where God is whipping water into a frenzy and lighting the woods on fire—*just with His voice*. And no human communication can do spiritual work in our heart like God can.

Go beyond this psalm for a moment and trace this voice in God's Word. The Bible starts with God speaking the world into existence (Genesis 1). At the Lord's command, the whole earth was flooded (Genesis 7). He speaks to Samuel, a child, in the night to show him what his work for God will be (1 Samuel 3). The Father's voice is heard as Jesus is baptized, commending Him (Matthew 3:17). Jesus cries, "It is finished!" as He accomplishes our salvation (John 19:30), and then, alive again from dead, He speaks peace to His fearful disciples (John 20:19–21). Jesus identifies Himself to an unbeliever named Saul—out loud while Saul is traveling—powerfully convicting him of sin and calling him to salvation (Acts 9). And at the end of the Bible, John describes the voice of the Lord Jesus like David does: "It sounded like a blast of a trumpet . . . [it] filled the air . . . like a roaring waterfall" (Revelation 1:10, 15).

Does your heart feel something when you contemplate God's verbal power? Psalm 29 guides our response to God when we realize His omnipotence. It tells us to praise Him for it! The psalm opens with a call to worship—telling us to "ascribe to the Lord glory and strength. Ascribe to the Lord the glory due His name; worship the Lord in the splendor of holiness" (vv. 1–2). When we understand the God Who can command nature like this, we bow, we yield, we recognize Him as Ruler. We say, "Lord! You are uniquely powerful and great. I am listening to Your voice."

Now, zoom out and view the psalm's closing picture of God—He is seated, majestic and great, and David prays for His blessing: "The Lord sits enthroned over the flood; the Lord sits enthroned as king forever. May the Lord give strength to his people! May the Lord bless his people with peace!"

Let the gospel convince you that the God Whose voice is all-powerful can also mightily save you.—ABBY

DAY 9

The Sinner's Plea for Mercy
READ PSALMS 32 & 51

"Wash me thoroughly from my iniquity, and cleanse me from my sin." PSALM 51:2

On October 31, 1517, Martin Luther nailed his *95 Theses* to the church door in Wittenberg, Germany, effectively starting the Protestant Reformation. Here's the first of his theses: "When our Lord and Master Jesus Christ said, 'Repent' (Matthew 4:17), He willed the entire life of believers to be one of repentance." Christians confess their sins as a constant rhythm of life, not just when we first trust Jesus as Savior. Why? Because we keep sinning, and while our salvation is settled once and for all at our conversion, our sweet fellowship with God waxes and wanes, hindered by our sin. We sin like David, so we need to repent like David. Psalms 32 and 51 show us how.

David was painfully aware of his sinfulness. David didn't shrug off his sin as a light thing. He mourned over it. He acknowledged to himself and to God that he was a sinner (51:3) and that his sin was rebellion against God (51:4). Yes, he sinned against Bathsheba and Uriah. But sin is especially treasonous because it is defiance against God. David owned his sin and its source in his deep-rooted sinfulness (51:5). When he said he was "conceived" in sin, he wasn't referring to some sin of his mother's. No, he was acknowledging that he was a sinner by nature, through and through. Put it this way: When you sin, don't pretend the sin was out of character, or unusual, or beneath you. Your sin is *you*, unvarnished. Own it. Confess it to God without excuse.

David was overwhelmed by conviction. Both Psalms 32 and 51 record David's conviction of sin—his uneasy conscience. Repulsed by his sin, David felt *spiritual* agony, including lost joy (32:1, 10; 51:8, 12) and lost fellowship with God (51:11). So severe was his grief over his sin that David felt *physical* agony as well, including lost sleep and physical illness (51:3–4). Have you experienced that kind of distress over your own sin?

David was deeply grateful for forgiveness. It's important to note that David's grief over his sin chased him *to* the Lord, not *away from* Him. Judas, on the other hand, grieved for his sin, but it led him to destroy himself, not to seek cleansing. Satan, ever the accuser (Revelation 12:10), will counterfeit true conviction, urging you to give up, forsake Christ, or even harm yourself. How different true conviction from the Holy Spirit is! True conviction chases you to Christ as your Savior, and it results in pardon. Notice David's joyful relief that the God he so recklessly offended is a God of forgiveness (32:1–2, 11; 51:8, 12). Yes, we are to grieve over our sins. But the goal of that grief is that we might come to know the joy of sin forgiven. The first word of Psalm 32, like the first word of Psalm 1, is *blessed* or *happy*! In his joyous relief, David committed himself anew to serve the Lord and point other sinners to Him (32:6–9; 51:13–17).

Psalms 32 and 51 point us forward to the saving work of Jesus Christ. Our sin isn't forgiven because we confess it so intensely, but because Jesus took our sins to the cross, bearing the punishment from God which our sins deserve. It's no mistake, then, that Romans 4:5–8 uses David's confession from Psalm 32:1–2 as proof of the salvation which faith in Jesus Christ brings. We are saved because God does not count our sins against us but has instead counted them against *Christ* (2 Corinthians 5:21).

Christian, when you sin—and you sin often—confess your sin to God, grateful for the cleansing power of Jesus' blood (1 John 1:7, 9). Rejoice that, even at your worst, you have Jesus as your Advocate with God and the Propitiation for your sins (1 John 2:1–2). But if you're not yet a Christian, I urge you to stop delaying. You are lost in sin, covered with filth, and in desperate need of cleansing. Repent of your sins and trust in Jesus as your only Savior today. Hurry!

Let the gospel move you to relieve your sin-pricked conscience through faith in Christ. —CHRIS

Don't Fret

DAY 10

READ PSALM 37

"Be still before the Lord and wait patiently for him; fret not yourself over the one who prospers in his way." PSALM 37:7

I know I'm not the only Christian who looks at prosperous unbelievers and feels jealousy. It frustrates us that wicked people seem to experience all the good stuff in this life, and it frustrated David, too. The opening of Psalm 37—"Don't envy or fret about evildoers"— resonates with us. We look at those who oppose Christianity but seem to have happy, beautiful lives, and we ask God, "How is this fair?" Here's what He says to us.

The "success" of the wicked is only temporary. Those who reject God may have their heyday now, but it's short-lived pleasure. Hear the insight of Robert Leighton, a pastor in the 1600s: "[God] often gives more of the world to those that shall have no more hereafter." Sure, unbelievers may be partying their way through life with a lot of money and fame— but they'll soon be gone (vv. 10, 36), withered like cut grass (vv. 2, 20). Their lives will "go up in smoke" (v. 20 NIV, James 4:14). God details their end, and it's horrible: The wicked will be "destroyed," "broken," and "cut off" (vv. 15, 17, 34, 38).

True success is found in God. Psalm 37 gives us God's solutions for discontentment.

1. *Don't fret.* God tells us three times (vv. 1, 7, 8) to stop agonizing about other people. He knows we're tempted to be upset, but He knows that feeding our frustration can turn us toward evil (v. 8). So he says, "Stop being angry about them."

2. *Live for God, not things.* It's easy to scroll through social media, stare at the wealth of this world, and let jealousy flourish. But God gives us alternatives to anger and envy: "Trust Me. Do good things for other people. Cultivate faithfulness to Christ—at your job, with your church, among your family. Find joy in Me—*just Me!* Roll all your concerns onto Me. And did I already mention it? *Trust Me*" (vv. 3–5).

3. *Be still and wait.* It's hard to sit quietly and not crave the life of your favorite celebrity. Modern life—i.e., instant everything—doesn't develop contentment or patience. But three times (vv. 7, 9, 34) God says, "Just wait and see what happens with the wicked. Just wait and see what great things I will give you." Psalm 37 paints a tragic end for evildoers, but we who trust in Christ's death have the glorious hope of the gospel. Just wait.

4. *Remember God's promises.* This psalm assures us that if we follow the Lord, we will shine (v. 6), we will receive an inheritance from God (vv. 9, 11, 22, 29, 34), and we will experience peace, stability, and *true* prosperity (vv. 11, 23, 31, 34). We're tempted by the lifestyle of the wicked, but God guarantees a *truly* good, eternal life for those who believe in His Son for salvation (Romans 8:29–30, 32; 1 Peter 1:3–5).

5. *Look at the past.* All of Christian history verifies God's care for His children. Christians don't have to beg: Our Father knows our circumstances and meets our needs (vv. 25–26). He loved us so much that He gave us His Son (John 3:16)!

6. *Hold on to truth.* Psalm 37 doesn't deny that bad people prosper. But it trumps that truth with better truths—that God loves justice (v. 28), that He won't ever leave us (v. 28), that we have His Word in our hearts to protect us (v. 31), and that He will help and deliver us (v. 40)! Recalling these realities helps us be content.

Martin Luther summarizes our struggle well: "And though this world, with devils filled, should threaten to undo us, we will not fear, for God has willed his truth to triumph through us" ("A Mighty Fortress Is Our God"). Do not fret. Take refuge in the Lord.

Let the gospel teach you to wait on God when you struggle with contentment in this life.
—ABBY

DAY 11

Turning to God in Sorrow
READ PSALM 39

"O Lord, make me know my end and what is the measure of my days; let me know how fleeting I am!" psalm 39:4

Gospel Meditations for the Hurting—another book in this devotional series—is one of my favorites. The authors have beautifully applied the hope of the gospel to all kinds of painful circumstances. Psalm 39 is set in that same kind of context. David is wading his way through a trial, and life feels bleak. In his grief, he writes a relatable poem-prayer to God about how short life is, affirming his hope in the Lord to help him navigate the hard times.

Silently working through grief (vv. 1–3)—David is having a rough time at the start of this psalm, but he chooses to bite his tongue. We don't know what has made him deeply sad (v. 2)—maybe son troubles? wife issues? battle losses? And he's in an environment where there are wicked people. Though he's tempted to vent about it, he doesn't want to "lose his testimony." This is doubly hard—to experience a trial but not have a safe place to talk through it. So, he resolves to watch his words and muzzle his mouth—so he won't sin in anger (vv. 1, 3). He is suffering silently (v. 2). *Takeaway:* Sometimes a period of silent, internal processing is helpful when we're grieving. Long-term, it is wise to talk to someone—especially God.

Realizing life is short (vv. 4–6)—Eventually, David turns to the Lord. In his sorrow, David has begun thinking about his brief time on this earth. Now, he opens up to God and prays, "Give me wisdom about how to use the little time I have!" (v. 4). To the eternal God, a human lifetime *is* like nothing—just a breath (v. 5, James 4:14). *Inhale. Exhale. And it's over.* And on top of the fact that life is short, death is sure! Yet, even in the face of this inevitability, we often live in denial, filling up our bank accounts like life will never end (v. 6). And though we might think that dwelling on death would *increase* our grief, David prays, "God, help me contemplate my mortality." *Takeaway:* It is humbling and good for us to meditate on how brief life is.

Hoping in God's deliverance (vv. 7–13)—David's great comfort in his sorrow is that the Lord is his hope. Halfway through, this psalm takes a wonderful turn: David proclaims a beautiful dependence on God. "Lord, my hope is in You" (v. 7)! Follow his thought process in this prayer. (And notice the gospel themes—salvation from sin and trust in the Lord.) He writes, "Lord, I depend on You to save me from my sin" (v. 8). "Lord, I believe You are the Author of this trial" (v. 9). "Lord, remove Your discipline from me" (v. 10). "Lord, hear and respond to my prayer" (v. 12). "Lord, in hope I walk through this life with You." (v. 12). What a great place to land in our grief—asking for deliverance, expressing humble dependence, affirming trust in the sovereignty of God. *Takeaway:* Our hope—in sin, affliction, or grief—is in the Lord Jesus, Who gave Himself for us.

If you are quietly suffering, Psalm 39 gives you amazing hope. Though you may struggle to express your grief, and though life can feel startlingly short, God is ever-present to hear your prayers. In hope, you can ask Jesus Christ to save you from your sin. And in hope, you can believe that He is sovereign over any affliction you are experiencing. Do not be afraid to trust the Lord. He has a purpose in your pain.

Let the gospel draw you to faith in Christ and give you hope in your suffering.—abby

A Song for the Wedding of All Weddings

DAY 12

READ PSALM 45

"With joy and gladness they are led along as they enter the palace of the king." PSALM 45:15

I've had the honor of officiating many weddings. With each ceremony, I am increasingly overwhelmed with emotion at the procession of the bride. As she walks down the aisle toward her groom, I smile from ear to ear, chills go up and down my spine, and tears fill my eyes. When I step back from such deeply moving moments and ask myself what's so stirring about them, I struggle a bit in explaining. It's not just that the gown and the music are beautiful. What moves me is that this woman and man are committing their lives to one another. They are making lifelong vows. And they are foreshadowing the wedding of all weddings.

The title of Psalm 45 indicates that it is "a love song." The beautiful poem describes a royal wedding, and the poet can't help but describe the supreme excellence of the Groom (vv. 1–9) as well as the majestic glory of the bride (vv. 10–15). The song's climactic moment is the procession of the bride and her attendants "down the aisle," as it were (v. 15).

Who is this King, and who is His bride? The most distinctive feature of this love song appears in verses 6–7. There the poet explains that the royal Groom is both God Himself and One anointed by God to rule on earth forever. Such a description must have led the author (as well as readers for several centuries) to scratch their heads in confusion: *I can understand that the coming king will be anointed by God, but how can he be called "God"?* Psalm 45 didn't begin to make sense until a virgin gave birth to a Son Who was fully God and fully human—both "Son of God and Son of Man!" (as the hymn "Fairest Lord Jesus," whose title echoes Psalm 45:2, so beautifully reminds us).

If the King extolled is none other than Jesus, then the bride described in Psalm 45 is none other than the church—all the sheep for whom the Great Shepherd laid down His life (Ephesians 5:22–33; John 10:11–16; Revelation 21–22). As the psalmist portrays this royal bride in verses 10–11, we learn that she has chosen to abandon her previous allegiances to her homeland and to her family. Instead, she is deciding to bow to Jesus because He is the One Who delighted in her so much that He gave His life for her. According to verse 12 (along with vv. 8–9, 16–17), Jesus's bride will be attended by people from every nation, and they will bring the wealth of their countries to Him (compare with Revelation 21:24). According to verses 13–14, Jesus's bride will be "all glorious" on the day of her wedding. She will be dressed in a beautiful gown which, no doubt, displays her King's spotless and invaluable obedience—a royal gift that, for all who believe, gets decisively credited to them and inevitably transforms their lives (Romans 3:21–4:8; Revelation 19:8). The bride will be presented to her King "in splendor, without spot . . . and without blemish" because of His cleansing, life-changing work in her (Ephesians 5:27). Then, according to verse 15, the bride will finally be presented to her Groom "with joy and gladness"—presented "before the presence of his glory with exceeding joy" (Jude 24 KJV).

Psalm 45 describes the wedding to which all other weddings faintly point. Just as every sacrificial lamb pointed to Jesus, every wedding points to the Great Wedding of Jesus and His bride! If you have turned from your waywardness and have yielded allegiance to King Jesus, then right now you are living between the marriage betrothal and the great wedding day. Christian, today is no time for you to be fooling around, allowing your heart to cheat on Him with worldly desires for pride, pleasure, and possessions (1 John 2:15–17). Now's the time for the bride to be counting down the days until "the wedding feast of the Lamb" and to be making preparations (Revelation 19:7).

Let the gospel keep fueling your admiration of and exclusive devotion to the King. —JOE

DAY 13

Money Won't Save Anyone
READ PSALM 49

"Truly no man can ransom another. . . . But as for me, God will redeem my life. He will snatch me from the power of the grave."
PSALM 49:7, 15 (ESV, NLT)

Ecclesiastes 7:2 pretty much flies in the face of our culture. Solomon writes that it's better to go to a funeral than a party. Really? Why? Because while a birthday bash lets us ignore our troubles, a funeral service appropriately sobers us. It reminds us that death is the end of the journey for *everyone*. This is also the wisdom of Psalm 49. "Listen," the sons of Korah say. "You may be rich, famous, and brilliant. But death is the great equalizer. Only God can ransom your soul."

The rich do not have ultimate power (vv. 1–9). We are often intimidated by powerful people (vv. 5, 16)—those who cheat us (v. 5) or brag about their wealth (v. 6). Money talks, and it can buy a lot in this world. But all the gold in Fort Knox can't do a single thing for your soul. Saving a soul from judgment in hell is "costly" (v. 8)—so expensive that "truly no [mere] man can ransom another or give to God the price of his life" (v. 7). And because we can't pay the price for our sin or anyone else's, God sent Jesus to pay for all our sin and ransom our souls eternally (1 Corinthians 6:20; Colossians 1:13–14). This is the power of the cross!

The rich will die like everyone else (vv. 10–14). There's no preferential treatment for the wealthy when they're six feet under. "The wise die; the fool and the stupid alike must perish" (v. 10). Death, the ghastly shepherd, guides everyone down the same one-way street to a new "home" in the grave (vv. 11, 14). Whether we're confidently rich or fearfully poor, we die just like animals (vv. 12, 20).

The rich cannot take their wealth with them (vv. 16–20). It's been cleverly said that there's no U-Haul behind a hearse. No matter how much we amass in this life, we leave it all to someone else (v. 10). "When [a rich man] dies he will carry nothing away," the psalm says (v. 17). We may be blessed financially or materially in life, but we will all one day lie buried in darkness, without any of our precious worldly goods (vv. 18–19).

But God . . . (v. 15). Most of Psalm 49 shoots holes in our worldly perspective on money. But the crux of the psalm is verse 15: "God will redeem my life. He will snatch me from the power of the grave." What a beautiful hope! Jesus came "to give His life as a ransom" (Matthew 20:28). Though no mere human can pay what we owe God for sinning against Him—*Jesus can!* And He already did, on the cross, to save you from eternal death.

As a high school teacher, I loved the study of William Cullen Bryant's poem "Thanatopsis"—Greek for "meditation on death." Bryant acknowledges that everyone—the "youth" and the "gray-headed man" alike—is marching toward "the silent halls of death." But, true to that Romantic era, Bryant's answer for our universal fear of dying is, first, to head for the great outdoors and listen to nature and, second, to take "comfort" that we'll be buried with the greats of history.

What a foolish idea of comfort—especially compared to this psalm's powerful truth that *God is our only Hope.* Your salvation from sin and death lies only in the "one mediator between God and men, the man Christ Jesus, who gave Himself as a ransom for all" (1 Timothy 2:5–6).

Let the gospel offer you hope through Jesus Who died to ransom you from death. —ABBY

Calm Amid Chaos

READ PSALM 55

"I am restless in my complaint and I moan." PSALM 55:2

DAY 14

Psalm 55:22 is a beautiful verse. I'm grateful for the invitation, echoed in 1 Peter 5:7, to find relief in Christ: "Cast your burden on the Lord, and he will sustain you; he will never permit the righteous to be moved." Lovely! But here's the thing. Psalm 55:22 is preceded by twenty-one verses and followed by another. When we rend it from its context, we blunt its power. God didn't give us soundbites; He gave us complete psalms and chapters and books. Context matters. If you like Psalm 55:22 on its own, you'll love it when you see it in its context. What drove David to cast his burdens on the Lord? What were his burdens? I'm glad you asked.

Psalm 55 is an inspired prayer—one of sixty laments in the book of Psalms. It's full of sorrow, confusion, and even anger. It teaches us how respond to trouble, heartbreak, and loss. If you've been there, you understand. If you haven't been there, you will be. So pay attention to the hardships that chased David to utter dependence on God.

David was surrounded by external foes (vv. 1–3, 9–11). David was encircled by enemies who wanted to destroy him. In response, he made his complaint to God, and he did so with shocking candor. Four times he begged God to pay attention to him: "Give ear to my prayer"; "hide not yourself from my plea" (v. 1); "attend to me" and "answer me" (v. 2). That's audacious—as though God were inattentive, much less *hiding* from us. But sometimes we feel this way, and God gives us permission to pray this way. Feeling oppression on every side, David asked God to help him (vv. 1–3) and to bring justice to his oppressors (vv. 9–11).

David was tormented by internal fears (vv. 4–8). Worse than being surrounded by enemies is being hounded by your own fears! David's language in this part of Psalm 55 is some of the rawest emotion in the Bible. Hear him, and feel his agony: "My heart is in anguish within me; the terrors of death have fallen upon me. Fear and trembling come upon me, and horror overwhelms me" (vv. 4–5). Have you experienced anguish, terror, fear, trembling, and horror? If so, you're not alone. David, a man after God's own heart, felt the same. You're not crazy. What David really wanted was relief and escape—so much so that he imagined being able to fly away from his problems (vv. 6–8). And we're not even finished.

David was abandoned by a false friend (vv. 12–15, 20–21). David was especially heartbroken that among his oppressors was someone who used to be his close companion. We don't know who it was, but David was betrayed on more than one occasion—by King Saul, by his counselor Ahithophel, and even by his own son Absalom. He expected to be hated by the Philistines, but "friendly fire" nearly broke his heart. You can't help but think of Jesus, David's greater Son, being betrayed by Judas, abandoned by His disciples, and denied by Peter. He understands.

David was desperate for God's deliverance (vv. 16–19, 22–23). Finally, after giving a catalogue of complaints, David called to God for help (v. 16). His prayers weren't eloquent; they were "complaints and groans" (v. 17). But he took them to the Lord, confident that God would hear and help him. Notice, however, that David didn't get immediate relief. This is important! After calling on God in verses 16–19, David again rehearsed his heartbreak in verses 20–21. Prayer isn't a magic potion that instantly removes your sorrows. Life continues to hurt, so you continue to pray. And now—finally, after all this anguish—we reach the climactic lesson in verses 22–23: "Cast your burden on the Lord." Whatever is battering you and breaking your heart, God can handle it. He hears. He helps. Run—or even limp—to Christ.

Let the gospel draw you toward Christ on your darkest days. —CHRIS

DAY 15

I Know God Is for Me

READ PSALM 56

"When I am afraid, I put my trust in you." PSALM 56:3

Fear is a universal human experience. We like to describe certain exceptionally daring people as "fearless," but the reality is that even those individuals fight their own phobias—whether spiders, dentist visits, enclosed spaces, public speaking.... Everyone has things that terrify them or trigger anxiety. But I love that Psalm 56 is just as universal when it offers us help for our fears *without* qualification. Psalm 56:4 does not limit which fears God can handle, as if He were only big enough to help with particular terrors for particular people. It just says that when we are afraid—for whatever reason—we can trust God. And because God knows we *all* fear things *all* the time, He has this psalm ready for us. "When your fear comes, do this: *Trust Me.*"

David shares a helpful personal illustration—a story of how he trusted God when he was fearful, "when the Philistines seized him in Gath." The details are in 1 Samuel 21: David is on the run, but he has foolishly sought safety in an enemy camp, so now he's a captive—definitely scary. I'm never worried about being captured by a neighboring army! But I can read Psalm 56 and say, "What do I learn from David's fear management?" Answer: I learn that one of David's habits of faith is to *pray when in trouble*. Here are the details—eight ways to pray when I'm scared.

1. ***Lord, I need grace, please.*** David starts with a petition (v. 1). He asks the Lord for favor, help, grace.

2. ***I am afraid.*** Even though God knows our situations, it is helpful for us to tell Him our hard realities. David says that he is scared because people (Saul? Philistines? others?) are against him. He feels trampled (v. 1); oppressed (v. 2); frustrated that people are twisting his words to mean things he didn't intend (v. 5); and fearful of their evil intents (v. 5), their attacks, and their plans to kill him (v. 6). Verbalize to God all the specifics of your fears.

3. ***God, I completely trust You.*** David affirms a couple things to the Lord (vv. 3, 4): that he is trusting God to help him and that he is not going to continue being afraid. Sometimes affirming our faith out loud to God helps us to believe and act.

4. ***What can people do, really?*** David asks a rhetorical question (v. 4). Answer: People can't do anything to truly threaten my life—not when I have God as my Protector. Tell God your worst-case scenarios and let Him assure you that, because of Jesus, you're secure forever.

5. ***Please judge them, God.*** David could go full revenge-mode here, but he leaves the judgment of his enemies with God (v. 7). This is a great biblical example of how to deal with those who wrong us (Romans 12:19).

6. ***God, You know.*** David repeats truth to himself during this mess: *God, You know my journey, my sorrows, my tears* (v. 8). God knows everything we face. Jesus sympathizes with your difficulties (Hebrews 4:15–16). And He cares (1 Peter 5:7).

7. ***I know You are for me, God.*** David reminds himself that he is not alone—that God is *with* him and *for* him (v. 9). This is big: the presence of God in my life trumps my fears (Hebrews 13:6; Romans 8:31–32).

8. ***God, You've rescued me before.*** David remembers the past (v. 13). If Jesus has saved you from sin, believe He can deliver you from present fears.

My trust in God can be expressed and enhanced when I pray. And my fears can be confronted and conquered when I pray. I have a God-designed prayer plan for dealing with the things that repeatedly make me afraid: Psalm 56.

Let the gospel provide a safe place of trust in God when you are tempted to fear. —ABBY

Cultivating a Thirst for God

DAY 16

READ PSALM 63

"My soul thirsts for you; my flesh faints for you." PSALM 63:1

What does it mean to thirst after God? Are Christians supposed to simply rest in what Jesus has done for us, or do we follow hard after God? Is our growth in Christlikeness automatic, or does it require effort on our part? Psalm 63 answers these and many more questions.

You may have an intimate relationship with the God of creation. Psalm 63 begins with two astounding words: *"Elohim, Eli."* *Elohim* is the first title we learn for God in Scripture: "In the beginning, *Elohim* . . ." (Genesis 1:1). It describes a God Who is so powerful that He can create everything that exists simply by speaking. *Elohim* is infinitely great, which makes the second word of Psalm 63:1 so remarkable: *Eli*. In English we translate it as *"my* God." Pause for a moment and take that in. The transcendent God Who is infinitely beyond us may be *owned* by us as a result of the gospel! No, we don't have authority over Him. But He's not just *a* God or *the* God, but *my* God. Beautiful!

You must seek God like one who is dying of thirst. David wants more of God. Notice the powerful image he uses to convey the intensity of his longing: "My soul thirsts for you; my flesh faints for you." Water is essential to life, not a luxury, and that was the intensity of David's desperation for more intimacy with God. Such longing grows out of the reality David confesses in verse 3: "Your love"—the love that caused God to give His Son as our Savior—"is better than life." Nothing else matters. And yet, we are prone to set God aside like some genie in a magic lamp—as though He were handy in a pinch but can otherwise be kept on the shelf. Psalm 63 urges you to repent of such arrogance and to deeply desire God. Yes, your intimacy with God begins by His gracious initiative. But it is deepened by your Spirit-enabled effort as you seek Him.

You will be satisfied with God—and still want more of Him. Verses 5–8 respond to David's *thirst for God* by declaring David's *satisfaction with God*. When we seek the Lord, He is eager to be found (Isaiah 55:6). When we draw near to God, He draws near to us (James 4:8). He's not aloof; He's not moody; He's not hiding from you. If you thirst for God, seek Him, and find Him, you will be more than satisfied. And yet, in a beautiful paradox, you will long for still more of Him. I wrote of this in a hymn called "Christ Is Sufficient":

> Nothing I've sought on earth satisfies; / I was designed to thirst after Christ.
> Beckoned by Him, "Drink and be filled." / I am content, yet yearn for Him still.

You are safe in God's hand, despite the schemes of your enemies. I love Psalm 63:8: "My soul clings to you." That's good. "Your right hand upholds me." Ah, that's much better! My security rests not on my grip but on God's (John 10:27–29). Although David is surrounded by enemies (vv. 9–11), he is safe, tucked under *Elohim's* protective wings (v. 7). So David can rejoice, even as he is slandered by His enemies. He has God—and God is enough.

A. W. Tozer's classic *The Pursuit of God* was the first book that really fed my soul. I especially identified with Tozer's gritty prayer that ends chapter 1: "I am ashamed of my lack of desire. O God, the Triune God, I want to want Thee; I long to be filled with longing; I thirst to be made more thirsty still." Maybe you relate to that as I did. You don't want God like you should. But you *want* to want Him. Great. That's a start. Ask God's forgiveness for your lack of desire (1 John 1:7, 9). Then ask God to both intensify and satisfy your thirst for Him. And He will.

Let the gospel draw you into ever deeper intimacy with God. —CHRIS

DAY 17

Quiet Worship
READ PSALM 65

"By awesome deeds you answer us with righteousness, O God of our salvation." PSALM 65:5

When I think of quiet worship experiences, my mind recalls beautiful outdoor places where I've been able to retreat, hear nothing but nature, and slow down to contemplate and praise the Lord. "There will be silence before You and praise in Zion, O God," David writes in Psalm 65:1 (NASB). Pulling away from the sounds of this chaotic world to find a calm space helps me regain an awe of the Lord and a reverence of Him. In the noise I cannot praise Him as I can in the silence.

God is the Prayer-Hearer. Having established a quiet worship context in Psalm 65:1, David moves to prayer. He addresses God as One Who hears our cries (v. 2), and he talks with the Lord about several things (vv. 2–4). He bemoans the very real fact of his fight with sin. He also remembers that God atones for and forgives sin—a truth especially precious to us who live after Jesus' sacrifice. He feels blessed that he has been chosen to come near to God, and he rejoices that worship in God's house is so satisfying and good.

And then David just keeps going. His praise song breaks open into a list of God-facts he wants to tell the Lord and recite for all of us. *You do awesome deeds, God* (v. 5). *You respond to us in righteousness* (v. 5). *You set up mountains and calm loud, stormy seas* (vv. 6–7). *You bring peace in human conflicts* (v. 8). *You make sunrise and sunset to shout beauty to us* (v. 8). Do you feel compelled to comment every time you see a beautiful sky?! I do!

God is the Master-Cultivator. Now David is on a roll, and he can't stop. He tells God, *You make it rain—sending water to the exact spots on Earth that need it* (v. 9). *You soften the ground, channel the rainwater toward dry regions, bringing fertility and growth and bounty* (vv. 10–11)! The reality is that we can live nearly anywhere in this world and see gorgeous landscapes and productive farms. I live in the American Midwest, where herds and crops are still thriving! Agribusiness is God's business, and successful harvest is from Him (v. 13).

So, by the last verse, David has offered a litany of praise to the Lord for His awesome deeds. I'm not an ecologist or a farmer at all by trade, but by the end of this psalm, I am in awe of how God blesses and cares for our planet. God's works in our world are mind-blowing. However, sometimes the natural world is terrifying, not beautiful. And to be honest, I can struggle with that. When 50,000+ die after an earthquake, and the news calls it an "act of God," it takes real trust in Him to call it "righteousness." It can be a challenge to keep worshiping Him.

Here's a conclusion that I've come to accept from Psalm 65: Every natural event demonstrates God's right-ness. *Everything* He does is just and worthy of worship. From the gentle rain, to the gorgeous sunrise, to the annual hurricane season—it *all* reminds us that God is greater than any turbulence in nature or humanity. In His great wisdom, He is the One Who knows what will most draw men and women to faith in Jesus. Whether it's His power to calm the sea (v. 7, Mark 4:35–41) or His power to curse a fig tree (Matthew 21:18–22), we "stand in awe of [His] signs" (v. 8).

Don't be afraid to get away to a quiet place and observe nature. Watch the ocean, drive through farm country, walk through a meadow, or hike a mountain. It may be exactly what you need—to think silently, ponder the truth of God's great power, pray for greater trust of His ways, and praise Him with the gratitude and worship He deserves.

Let the gospel quiet you, show you your Creator, and move you to worship Him. —ABBY

All the Peoples
READ PSALM 67

"Let the peoples praise you, O God; let all the peoples praise you!" PSALM 67:3

I know flying isn't for everyone, but ever since I was bit by the travel bug, I've been hooked. By 23, I'd seen Canada, Colombia, a whole bunch of Europe, and Australia—it's a season of my life that I feel very privileged to have experienced. And while every part of my globetrotting was educational, one of the main takeaways for me as a believer was that God and Christianity are global. The gospel is multicultural, not American. While there are separate nations and rulers on earth, there is really only one universal King, and He will be praised internationally. Psalm 67 trumpets this truth: The world—all of it—is called to experience God's salvation and rejoice in it!

Goal #1: Grace for us. It almost seems audacious to ask the God of the whole universe to be gracious to us. We're ridiculously small in comparison to Him—just grasshoppers (Isaiah 40:22). Meanwhile, God is great, magnificent, supreme, unfathomable (Psalm 145). And so, to say, "May God be gracious to us and bless us and make his face to shine upon us" (v. 1) is quite the prayer! But God's instruction in Numbers 6:24–26 and similar words in many psalms show us that this request is appropriate (Psalms 6, 9, 25, 31, 41, 51, 57, 80, 86). And look at the beautiful biblical idiom layered into this prayer: that God would *shine His face* on us. It's a very human image: Our faces beam when we're happy—we smile when we're pleased with someone. So, in anthropomorphic language, David is asking God to show His favor. (See Deuteronomy 31:17–18, Isaiah 59:2, and Micah 3:4 where God hides His face, and by implication, His blessing.) Today, no matter who you are or where you live on this globe, you can ask for God's grace and blessing on your life.

Goal #2: Global evangelism. We are so inundated with information about Christianity in our country that we can easily forget that not everyone in this world knows about God or His saving power (v. 2). But this psalm lays out a life goal for us—to know Him ourselves and make sure others know Him, too. Almost every verse of this psalm touches on the *global* scope of the gospel. *Where* should God's way be known? On earth—*all* of it! *Who* should learn of God's saving power and fear Him? *All* nations, *all* the peoples, *all* the ends of the earth (vv. 2, 3, 5, 7). Maybe you've thought of the Bible as a Jewish storybook. It's not. God chose Israel in order to bless "all the peoples" (v. 7) with a Savior—Jesus Christ. In Isaiah 45:21–22, God calls the whole world to salvation in one Savior: "There is no other god besides me, a righteous God and a Savior. . . . Turn to me and be saved, all the ends of the earth!"

Goal #3: God's glory. You can't miss this psalm's celebratory tone! The words "praise" and "be glad" and "sing for joy" (vv. 3–4) give an attitude of joy to the prayer. Think about how excited the world gets about the Olympics. That event thrills us, in part, because we see people coming together, uniting around activities that they can enjoy despite all their cultural differences. But heaven! We ain't seen nothin' yet. This will be all the saved, from all eras since the beginning of time, uniting together around—not track or swimming or skiing—but God Almighty! The global praise of God one day is going to astound us. The book of Revelation describes this universal worship of the future:

> "A great multitude that no one [can] number, from every nation, from all tribes and peoples and languages, standing before the throne and before the Lamb, . . . crying out with a loud voice, 'Salvation belongs to our God who sits on the throne, and to the Lamb!'" (Revelation 7:9–10)

Let the gospel cause you to pray that people from every part of this world will know God's saving power through Jesus Christ. —ABBY

DAY 19
The Restlessness of a Rubbernecker
READ PSALM 73

"But as for me, my feet had almost stumbled, my steps had nearly slipped." PSALM 73:2

Do you know what a *rubbernecker* is? It's a term traffic reporters use as they fly over congested highways and warn commuters about the stalled interstates they'll want to avoid. Rubberneckers back up traffic by slowing down and craning their necks to *look* at accidents. Asaph's rubbernecking in Psalm 73 got him in trouble. He knew theoretically that God is good to His people (v. 1). Ah, but his own experience seemed like an exception to that rule: "But as for me . . ." (v. 2). His looking at the successes of the wicked rather than at the grace of God almost caused him to have a spiritual fender-bender. Asaph's experience is one we all share, and we need his inspired counsel.

Focusing on temporary injustice is demotivating and dangerous. Psalms of lament sometimes grow out of the oppression of an enemy (like Psalm 3) or the treachery of a presumed friend (like Psalm 55). But in Psalm 73, Asaph was tormented by a yahoo on a yacht: "I was envious of the arrogant when I saw the prosperity of the wicked" (v. 3). The word *prosperity* is actually the world's best-known Hebrew word: *shalom*. It seemed to Asaph that crime pays, that life isn't fair, that sin brings peace. Verses 4–12 recount his frustration in detail, but his summary will suffice: "Behold, these are the wicked; always at ease, they increase in riches" (v. 12).

Asaph was in a dangerous frame of mind. The apparent ease of the wicked made Asaph conclude that his own pursuit of godliness was a waste of time (vv. 13–15). Such mercenary motives make religion a means to an end. Asaph was flirting with the heresy of the prosperity gospel. *Aren't God's people supposed to be more successful than the wicked?* Actually, the Bible's answer is a resounding "no." The fact that godliness invites persecution isn't exactly the fine print of Scripture. Jesus' parable in Luke 16:19–31 makes the case well. History is filled with rich people who "feast sumptuously every day" (v. 19) while the godly are covered with sores, eating crumbs, and hanging out with dogs (v. 20). Such inequities exasperated Asaph, and they almost led him to ruin.

Focusing on eternal justice is encouraging. Thank God for the "But" that comes in verse 16. Asaph finally came to his senses, and it was time in God's presence that set him straight (v. 17). He learned that the "pleasures of sin" are fleeting (Hebrews 11:25). The ungodly will slip and fall, if not on earth then in eternity (vv. 18–19). The Lord is keeping tabs (contrary to Asaph's grumbling in v. 11), and He will bring the wicked to justice (v. 20). Asaph recognized his brutish and beastly stupidity, and he repented (vv. 21–22). We need this, too, like a splash of cold water in the face. We can expect a life of injustice now. Our "best life" is later, and our reward in glory is infinitely greater than our current suffering (Romans 8:18). Conversely, the temporary pleasures of the wicked are not worthy to be compared with the agonies that await them. Believe it.

Focusing on God Himself is soul-satisfying. The real solution to Asaph's rubbernecking wasn't a promise that godliness pays in the end. Again, that's too shallow and short-sighted a motive. No, our ultimate prize is *God Himself*. Asaph moved beyond questions of inequity to find his true hope and pleasure in God, not God's gifts. He delighted in God's presence and counsel (vv. 23–24). He learned that God Himself is enough: "There is nothing on earth that I desire besides you" (v. 25). Yes, Asaph's frailty would continue (v. 26a), but he found in God the strength his heart needed and the portion—the *inheritance*—that was more valuable than anything the world could offer. Asaph learned the truth of Philippians 1:21: "To live is Christ, and to die is gain." Rescued from his self-deception, Asaph ended his miniature biography with a sobering contrast: Those who are far from God will perish (v. 27), but those who are near to God will be safe in His refuge—now and forever (v. 28).

Let the gospel make you content with Christ rather than envious of the wicked. —CHRIS

Looking Back to Look Forward

DAY 20

READ PSALM 78

"... that the next generation might know them." PSALM 78:6

History was a subject I endured in high school rather than enjoyed. History was riddled with dead people, dates, and documents—blah, blah, blah. Now I wish I could go back and do it all again. I *love* history, especially when it's told by masters like the late David McCullough. Well, Psalm 78 is a history lesson. But it's much more! Looking at God's work in the past is a vital way to prepare us and our children for the present and future.

A Summary of Israel's History—Psalm 78 gives a one-chapter summary of Israel's history, very like the early sermons in Acts do (Acts 3, 7, 13). The psalmist rehearses God's choice of Jacob (v. 5). He recalls God's deliverance of Israel from Egypt—including the Red Sea, guidance through the wilderness, and miraculous provisions of water, manna, and quail (vv. 12–16, 23–31). He reviews the ten plagues (vv. 42–53) and the conquest of the Promised Land (vv. 54–55), climaxing with God's provision of David as Israel's greatest king (vv. 67–72). But sadly, intermingled with the records of God's goodness are cautionary tales of the people's sinfulness (vv. 10–11, 17–22, 30–33, 40–42, 56–64). Their repentance was occasional and short-lived (vv. 34–39). Yet, again and again, God showed His people undeserved mercy (vv. 38, 65–66)—a mercy that would climax in His gift of the Messiah to be their Savior. The summary of the psalm is God's faithfulness amid faithlessness.

Essential Lessons for Us Today—History can feel irrelevant to everyday life. Alexander the Great's empire was divided among his four generals.... *So what?!* But Psalm 78's history is germane to the most important aspects of our lives. Here are a few essential lessons:

Biblical history is intended to give us real-life examples of God's kindness. Yes, Scripture gives us lists of people who did exploits by faith (Hebrews 11). But even Scripture's *best* men were *but* men; they were exceptionally flawed people, and yet God was kind to them. The Bible's lesson is not that we should endeavor to be heroes. Rather, it's that we should place our confidence in Christ—the Bible's one true Hero—depending on Him to rescue us and help us.

Biblical history is intended to give us real-life examples of sinful rebellion and its consequences. First Corinthians 10:6–13 teaches that Old Testament events "took place as examples for us, that we might not desire evil as they did" (v. 6). It warns us against idolatry, immorality, ingratitude, and grumbling. When we read Israel's stories, we should be mindful of our own frailties, and even more mindful of Christ's provision.

God wants His people to know their Bibles. God doesn't want mindless obedience. He expects every generation to know and apply His Word. Christianity encourages thinking and understanding, unlike religions which elevate the clergy and neglect the foolish laity. Biblical truth isn't just for scholars or pastors—it's for every believer.

God is deeply interested in children. One key lesson of Psalm 78 is that God's people are expected to teach His works to our children. "Our fathers told us" of God's works (v. 3), and we are to teach those same truths "to the coming generation" (vv. 4–8; Psalm 145:4). Above all, we must urge our children to know and love Christ (Ephesians 6:4).

The book of Judges describes a low point in Israel's history. Judges 2:10 gives the reason: "And there arose another generation ... who did not know the LORD or the work that he had done for Israel." No wonder Scripture repeatedly commands us—even through the Lord's Table—to remember what God has done and to teach it to the coming generations.

Let the gospel motivate you to look back at God's might and mercy so that you can cultivate faith in your heart and the hearts of your children.—CHRIS

DAY 21

Tick, Tick, Tick
READ PSALM 90

"Establish the work of our hands." PSALM 90:17

I hear a stopwatch ticking in my head whenever I read Psalm 90. It's the oldest psalm, written by Moses sometime around 1400 B.C.—400 years before David's psalms and around 1000 years before the last psalms were penned. Fittingly, it's all about time. It talks about "days" five times (vv. 4, 9, 12, 14, 15) and "years" four times (vv. 4, 9, 10, 15). It refers to God's faithfulness through "all generations" (v. 1) and His existence "from everlasting to everlasting" (v. 2). *Tick, tick, tick.* Hear it? It's a sobering psalm, and it has timeless lessons for us.

Our time is fleeting. Moses doesn't just opine about time. Rather, he contrasts the brevity of human life with the eternity of God. The psalm begins with a thankful reflection on God's enduring care for His people: "Lord, you have been our dwelling place in all generations" (v. 1). It describes God's existence before creation; God is the uncaused Cause of everything we see, from mountains to planets (v. 2a). It reminds us that God is unchanging: "From everlasting to everlasting you are God" (v. 2b). It tells us that a millennium passes for God just as a night passes for us (v. 4; 2 Peter 3:8).

Notice the contrast in verse 4: Moses shows how time rules over us, whereas God is ageless. Our short time on earth is compared to dust (v. 3; Genesis 3:19), to clutter swept away by a flood (v. 5), to a passing dream (v. 5), to grass (vv. 5–6; Isaiah 40:6–8; Job 14:1–2), and to a sigh (v. 9). On average, we live for maybe seventy or eighty years, and even that brief time flies (v. 10). As James 4:14 puts it, "You are a mist that appears for a little time and then vanishes." Life itself is a fatal condition.

Our guilt is glaring. We are under a death sentence, and not just because we are mortal. Our sin is unhidden to God (v. 8), and it has earned for us His just anger and wrath. This isn't a passing problem; *anger* and *wrath* are mentioned five times in verses 7, 9, and 11. In fact, verse 15 seems to indicate that Psalm 90 was written in response to some national calamity brought on by Israel's rebellion—and there are countless episodes in their checkered history that could be candidates. But let's focus on ourselves. *Our* sinfulness places *us* under God's wrath. Where can we find deliverance? I've always read in verse 11 a hint toward the cross. We can't impose Jesus into the text—but follow me: Moses asks a seemingly rhetorical question: *Who has known the power of God's infinite wrath?* The question expects a negative answer: nobody! But the New Testament Christian knows that there *is* one Person Who has tasted and drained the undiluted wrath of God—the Lord Jesus, the Propitiation for our sins, the perfect Sacrifice Who absorbed the full rage of God which we deserve (1 John 2:2; 4:10). For the Christian, God has no wrath left; Jesus has exhausted it. Jesus is the sinner's only hope.

Our work may be meaningful. We get but one life. That's it. There's no reset button. So Moses exhorts us in verses 12–18 to use our time wisely: "Teach us to number our days that we may get a heart of wisdom" (v. 12). He asks God for mercy, for gladness in place of mourning, and for an ongoing demonstration of God's power (vv. 13–16). Perhaps climactically, he asks for God's favor to be on His people (v. 17). In other words, he asks for my favorite biblical concept: *grace*. And one result of God's grace is that our short lives need not be wasted. He prays—twice, for good measure—that God will "establish the work of our hands" (v. 17). In God's mercy, our work (which, in reality, is *His* work) can mean something! We can do even mundane work "as for the Lord" (Colossians 3:23–24). We can point those within our sphere of influence to Christ. We can even leave a legacy that outlives us in time and eternity. *Use us, Lord, by Your grace and for Your glory, for as long as we have breath!*

Let the gospel drive you to use your fleeting life in the service of your Savior. —CHRIS

Nothing *Ultimately* Bad Will Happen
READ PSALM 91

DAY 22

"No evil shall be allowed to befall you, no plague come near your tent." PSALM 91:10

Anxiety is among the most pressing of human problems. People deal with unease over all kinds of present problems such as financial debt, marital distance, wayward children, school deadlines, spiritual guilt, work load, and bodily pain. And people deal with worry over potential problems—problems that don't yet exist and which may or may not materialize. These potential worries include unknowns: *What if the market collapses? What if that person never changes? What if I lose my job? What if I never get married? What if the lab report comes back malignant? What if I fail again?*

Psalm 91 is written for the anxious. It's designed by God to help His vulnerable children feel safe. It's a song of refuge, describing what it's like to trust God when your life is threatened by various dangers (vv. 3–13). Throughout the song, God repeatedly likens Himself to a "storm shelter" in which His children hide for safety when under a tornado watch. He describes Himself as a strong fortress that protects from invading armies, as a battle shield that protects from incoming arrows, and as a bird that uses its wings to protect its young from predators. Psalm 91 assures you, if you are trusting the Lord, that "no evil shall be allowed to befall you" (v. 10). How should you understand that promise? It sounds like God is promising that He won't allow anything bad to happen to you. Is that so?

What Psalm 91 Doesn't Mean. A massive clarification is in order. Psalm 91 can't be promising that nothing bad will *ever* happen to those who trust God. That should be fairly obvious since the whole psalm itself repeatedly assumes that God's people will endure all sorts of trouble. But this elucidation was made with crystal clarity when Satan misinterpreted this passage in his temptation of Jesus. When Satan tried to make God the Son rebel against God the Father, Satan quoted (and misinterpreted) Psalm 91 (Matthew 4:5–7). The devil urged Jesus to demand that God miraculously and publicly prevent anything bad from happening to Him. But Jesus resisted Satan's temptation, and responded by humbly submitting Himself to God's will, including all the suffering that lay ahead. So, believer, you must not interpret Psalm 91 like Satan! Don't ever demand that God prove His love for you by never letting anything bad happen to you. That's not what this song is promising, and such a false belief could ruin your faith.

What Psalm 91 Does Mean. In Psalm 91, God is promising that nothing *ultimately* bad will happen to you. Christian, since Jesus bore the wrath of God that you deserved, the worst thing that could ever happen to you—experiencing "punishment with the wicked" or dying "the second death"—will never happen to you (v. 8; Revelation 20:14–15). Although you may face "tribulation, or distress, or persecution," there is absolutely nothing "in all creation [that] will be able to separate [you] from the love of God in Christ Jesus our Lord" (Romans 8:35–39).

If Psalm 91 were a fireworks display of assurance, then verses 14–16 would be the grand finale. There God promises ultimate blessings to the person who loves Him and keeps relying on Him. Listen to the glorious explosions! *You'll be forever safe! All your cries will be answered! You'll never be alone! You'll be forever satisfied! You'll be forever saved!* Believer, there's coming a day when you'll experience God's complete salvation from every effect of sin and death—when all your tears will be wiped away and all your trials will be in the past (Revelation 7:15–17). Since that day of ultimate salvation is coming, don't give in to sinful distrust and anxiety today. Instead, sing Psalm 91, confident that temporary sorrows will yield to ultimate triumph.

Let the gospel's promises stabilize you through today's trials and tomorrow's unknowns.—JOE

DAY 23

Worship & Witness
READ PSALM 96

"For great is the Lord, and greatly to be praised." PSALM 96:4

Psalm 96 is one of my favorites. It's a jubilant psalm, urging us to worship God and rehearsing for us God's many excellencies. It's also a missional psalm, foreshadowing the global reach of the gospel a thousand years after the psalm was written. And it looks even further into the future, anticipating the final triumph of good over evil and God over everything at Jesus' second coming. This is rich!

Our God deserves to be worshiped by His people. The psalm begins with a call to worship. Three times in the first two verses it commands the people of God to "sing!" The command to sing is the most frequent command in the Bible. But the psalms don't call for mindless emotion. Rather, they tell us *why* we should sing to the Lord by drawing our attention to His character with laser-like focus. He is our Savior (v. 2). He is glorious, and He does wondrous works (v. 3). He is great (v. 4). He is contrasted with worthless idols (v. 5). He is a God of splendor, majesty, strength, and beauty (v. 6). He is a glorious God, as the psalm tells us three times (vv. 3, 7, 8). He is holy and fearsome (v. 9). He reigns in heaven now (v. 10), and He will one day rule on earth with perfect justice, equity, and faithfulness (vv. 10b, 13). And so, we give Him the glory He is due (v. 8)—an impossible command we will spend eternity trying to fulfill.

Our God deserves to be worshiped by all people. Many psalms exalt the Lord for His perfections. But Psalm 96 tells us that God is so great that He deserves to be praised by more and more worshipers. That's the point of Psalm 96:4: "For great is the Lord, and greatly to be praised." Is that calling for louder singing? Better hymns? No, although both are worthy goals. In context, Psalm 96:4 is calling for *more worshipers*— God is so great that we need to invite unbelievers to praise Him with us. The psalm invites Gentiles to join in the praise of Jehovah, and it does so again and again. Reread the psalm and notice its inclusion of *all* people (vv. 1, 3, 5, 7, 9, 10, 13). God's people are commanded to declare His glory all over the world so that all people will believe in Jesus, be saved, and join in praising Him around the throne (v. 3; Revelation 5:9–10). I love the way the hated Samaritans grasped this truth in John 4:42: Jesus isn't just the Savior of the Jews (or Westerners, or Americans). *He's the Savior of the world!*

Our God will one day be worshiped by all creation. God's redemption plan doesn't end with the salvation of fallen sinners. Instead, it's a cosmic plan. God is going to save the entirety of creation, including the plants and animals which were dragged under the curse by Adam's initial sin (Genesis 3). Romans 8:18–25 says that creation *groans*. God's perfect world has been marred, and creation feels it—from natural catastrophes to disease and hunger and death. Ah, but Romans 8 also says that creation *waits* (v. 19). The mess the first Adam made is going to be fixed entirely by Jesus—the Second Adam. Our fallen world, like fallen sinners, needs a rebirth. And its rebirth is coming! The climax of Scripture is when Jesus condemns Satan and sinners (Revelation 20), makes all things new (Revelation 21), and reverses the curse (Revelation 22:3). Psalm 96 anticipates this, whimsically and beautifully. Rather than groaning, all creation will worship (vv. 11–12). The heavens will be glad, the earth will rejoice, the sea and its creatures will roar, fields and their varied animals will exult, and even the trees will sing with us when the Judge returns to remake this fallen world and judge it with equity.

That is how great our God is. *That* is how extensive His salvation plan is. And *that* is why worshiping and witnessing are inseparably linked. It is every Christian's duty to announce Jesus's saving work to the lost. Go!

Let the gospel inspire you to take the light of Jesus to those who languish in darkness, all over the world.—CHRIS

The Chart-Topper
READ PSALM 110 & HEBREWS 7

DAY 24

"Sit at my right hand, until I make your enemies your footstool." PSALM 110:1

Psalm 110 is the psalm that was most quoted by Jesus and His apostles. In the first generation of Christians, it was "the chart-topper." The New Testament writers refer to it more than twenty times. They loved this psalm. Let's find out why.

One thousand years before Jesus was born in Bethlehem, God allowed King David to listen in on a divine conversation. David heard God the Father speak to God the Son and promise to give Him eternal, worldwide dominion. David reported that although the Messiah would be a King from David's own dynasty, David would be this King's servant. David also reported that the Messiah, though from David's tribe of Judah (and not from the priestly tribe of Levi), would be the eternal Priest—the One Who could forever reconcile sinners with God. What remarkable prophetic details! Yet, here's the most foundational feature of the song's prophecy: Before God's Messiah would conquer all of God's enemies, He would be enthroned—He would "sit at [the Father's] right hand." Consider how Psalm 110 permeates the New Testament.

Before and after the crucifixion, Jesus and His apostles quoted Psalm 110. During the week before He died, the Lord Jesus quoted Psalm 110 on two occasions (see Matthew 22:41–45 and 26:63–64). Jesus clearly understood that the psalm was about Him. Peter, Jesus's lead apostle, was also convinced that Psalm 110 referred to Jesus. Just days after witnessing Jesus's crucifixion, resurrection, and ascension, Peter preached that Psalm 110 had been fulfilled when Jesus ascended into heaven—when Jesus was "exalted at the right hand of God" (Acts 2:32–36). We must recognize what Peter preached to the Jews who crucified Jesus: that forgiveness is found only in repenting of our sin and submitting to the ascended King!

To suffering Christians, the writer of Hebrews preached Psalm 110. Did you know that the letter to the Hebrews is basically an extended sermon on Psalm 110? The letter was written to ethnic Jews who were facing horrible suffering for their decision to follow Christ. To encourage their perseverance, the author continually reminded these weary believers that Jesus reigns—that God's chosen King and Priest is enthroned just as Psalm 110 had predicted (Hebrews 1:3, 13; 5:6, 10; 6:20; 7:1–8:1; 10:11–14; 12:2). So, Christian, endure every hardship with eyes fixed on the ascended King!

In discipling churches, Paul used Psalm 110. The apostle Paul repeatedly referred to Psalm 110:1 in his letters to the churches. According to Paul, the fact that Jesus has ascended and taken a seat at the right hand of His Father should shape every Christian's life in fundamental ways. Jesus' triumph should lead every believer to a strong sense of security, to an aggressive pursuit of virtue, to an enduring commitment to Jesus' church, and to a steadfast hope in the face of death (Romans 8:34; Colossians 3:1; Ephesians 1:19–23; and 1 Corinthians 15:24–28). So, believer, live as if your life is forever united with the King Who is presently enthroned at God's right hand—because He is there, and you are His!

If all of the psalms that prophesy about Jesus were compiled onto a single album of "greatest hits," Psalm 110 would be the signature song. Of all the inspired songs that Jesus and His apostles loved to sing, Psalm 110 is number one. Its music shaped the lives of first-century Christians and fueled their endurance. Christian, let the truth of Psalm 110 anchor you like it anchored the early church.

Let the gospel of the King's ascension be your soul's unshakable foundation.—JOE

DAY 25

The Bible in a Nutshell
READ PSALM 117

*"Great is his steadfast love toward us, and the faithfulness of the L*ORD *endures forever. Praise the L*ORD*!"* PSALM 117:2

Psalm 117 is the shortest song in the Bible's hymnbook. It's small, like a nutshell. And like a nutshell, Psalm 117 is potent, containing the seed of a mighty tree. This little chorus packs into two verses of poetry the overarching message of all sixty-six books of the Bible! In verse 1, the psalm calls people of every nation to praise the Lord. Verse 2 explains why: because the Lord's covenant-keeping love is great and eternal. These two simple verses—focused on God's great love and the international worship it inspires—are a tightly condensed summary of what God is doing through the gospel.

I've stated that Psalm 117 is a synopsis of the whole Bible. Let me explain how by posing a half-dozen questions that walk through biblical history.

1. After Adam and Eve treacherously broke their covenant relationship with God, why didn't God just obliterate humanity? Why did He pursue Adam and Eve in their shame? And why, even as He punished them, did He promise to eventually send a Man to end sin and death?

2. After judging most of rebellious humanity at the Flood and after dividing defiant humanity into many languages and nations at Babel, why did God make promises to idolatrous Abram to bless every nation through his Offspring?

3. After Jacob, Abraham's grandson, lived for years as a deplorable brother, husband, and father, why didn't God wipe out this deceiver instead of sparing his life? (Hint: Look up Genesis 32:9–11.)

4. After Jacob's descendants were delivered from Egypt and yet responded with gross idolatry at the base of Mount Sinai, why didn't God terminate these rebellious people? (Hint: Look up Exodus 34:6–7, one of the most significant passages in the Bible.)

5. After a thousand years in which Israel and her kings continually sought the help of foreign gods and nations through idolatry and polygamy, why didn't God just exterminate this stubborn nation? (Hint: Look up Nehemiah 9:31–32.)

6. After millennia of human treachery, why did God send His one and only Son into the world to be crucified—to endure the punishment that rebels deserved? (Hint: Look up John 1:14 and compare it with Exodus 33:18–34:7.)

Why? *Why?* Psalm 117 answers: Because God's faithful love is *great!* (v. 2). When the poet describes God's covenant-keeping love as "great," he isn't using a generic term that means something like "massive," although that's certainly true. Instead, the writer is using a specific term that means something like "all-conquering" or "prevailing over all." (Take a minute to see how this term *great* is repeatedly translated in Genesis 7:18–20.) Psalm 117 rejoices in God because He will not allow sin and death to prevail on earth! The all-conquering grace of Jesus' atonement will prevail in the lives of all who have taken refuge in Him. Human history will end with shouts of praise from people of every nation, glorifying the grace of the Lamb that will crush the dominion of sin and death. That's the Bible in a nutshell. That's human history in a nutshell: God's covenant-keeping love will prevail!

Let the gospel's all-prevailing power lead you today to praise the Lord and to pray for the gospel's advance among the nations.—JOE

"Read Your Bible—Pray Every Day"

DAY 26

READ PSALM 119 (or any portion of it)

"Oh that my ways may be steadfast in keeping your statutes!" PSALM 119:5

Most Christians know that Psalm 119 is long—*really* long. But do you know that each of its 176 verses unites Scripture and prayer? That's what you'll see if you step back from this epic composition and view it as a panorama—the way you look at a vast mountain range. Every line is a prayer to God that focuses on His Word. The inspired poet keeps praying, "Lord, I love your Word! Please keep me faithful to Your Word. Help me to be faithful as I wait on You to fulfill every promise in it." Those three expressions should be instructive for every Christian who desires to live a life of prayer-saturated Bible reading and Word-filled prayer.

In prayer, express to God how much you love His Word. The songwriter uses many different terms for the Scriptures, including "law," "testimonies," "rules," and "promises," to name a few. He also expresses his love, using various terms of delight and longing. Throughout the psalm, he keeps saying, "I'm so happy when I read Your law! Your testimonies, God, thrill me! I absolutely love Your law!" (vv. 14, 16, 24, 35, 47, 70, 97, 113, 119, 127, 140, 143, 159, 163, 167, 174). When is the last time that you told God in prayer how much you *love* His Word? When is the last time you told God how much you *long for* His Word? Such prayers should characterize your life.

In prayer, beg for God to help you obey His Word. Loving the Bible is part of the new nature God has put within believers. According to the terms of the New Covenant, every person who has been reconciled to God through faith in Jesus starts to crave the Bible—we want to know and obey it (Hebrews 8:10; 1 John 5:3). Christians instinctively hunger for God's Word like newborn babies hunger for milk (1 Peter 2:2). Yet, when it comes to feeding on the Bible and walking according to the Bible, Christians can have bad habits. The writer of Psalm 119 often found himself lethargic and weak. He knew that understanding and obeying the Bible requires help from God Himself. So, he constantly prayed for it. Do you beg God every day to feed you with His Word, to forgive you for so frequently disobeying it, and to prevent you from living hypocritically? Express in prayer how much you want to live a life that conforms to the Word!

In prayer, wait on God to fulfill every promise of His Word. The poet continually begs God, "Fulfill all Your promises! Rescue me and comfort me as You've promised to do! Preserve me till I can praise You for fulfilling all Your promises!" (See, for example, vv. 41, 82, 123, 133, 174.) Wonderful promises saturate God's Word—promises that God will never forsake us, that He will complete the good work He's begun in us, and that His chosen King will bring justice and peace on earth. Yet, such promises can feel so distant to afflicted believers. Those who are suffering often feel that God is not near, that personal failure may win out, and that the world will never be set right. If that's you today, cling to God's promises through personal, persevering prayer. It's not enough simply to know what God promises in the Word; you must prayerfully plead for God to fulfill every promise He has made (Luke 18:7).

Every verse of the twenty-two stanzas of this monumental song models the crucial combination of the Word and prayer. Christian, live a Psalm-119 kind of life. Experience the ups and downs with an open Bible. And let all of its history, its laws, and its prophesies drive you to commune with God Himself in prayer. Tell Him how much His Word delights you, beg Him for help to obey it, and wait on Him to fulfill every promise in it.

Let the gospel that reconciled you to God keep driving your prayerful dependence on His Word.—JOE

DAY 27

Mature Humility

READ PSALM 131

"O Lord, my heart is not lifted up." PSALM 131:1

Have you heard of the book I wrote? It's called *The Ten Most Humble People, and How I Taught the Other Nine.* At first glance, Psalm 131 seems to begin like that joke. David prays, "Lord, my heart is not proud" (NLT). Was David arrogant to tell God how humble he was? No. He was manifesting humility in its most mature form. Let's think about the virtue of humility from the ground up.

Do we need humility? Humility isn't natural for anyone. From the time we're infants, we think that the world should revolve around us—our needs, our schedules, our demands. As we grow older, it's typical for us to think of ourselves as fairly strong, fairly good, and fairly important. And as we mature into adulthood, we often assume that the course of our lives is primarily determined by our own decisions. Each of those instinctive self-assessments is an illusion.

What is humility? Humility is an accurate assessment of ourselves in relation to God, especially in comparison to His unique greatness and His undeserved grace. We have a clear view of ourselves when we recognize that we are creatures who are totally dependent on our life-giving Creator. Further, we're thinking accurately when we recognize that we are rebels against God who can be rescued from our condemnation only through the redemption He offers. We can't save ourselves! We must humbly trust Jesus.

Where does humility begin? Humility is sourced in Jesus, and it takes root in the lives of those who turn to Him. King Jesus was perfectly humble—He lived to please His Father and to serve others. In humble love He submitted Himself to the humiliation of crucifixion (Philippians 2:1–11). Though He knew that His Father had the power to deliver Him from suffering, Jesus committed Himself to silently endure whatever "Abba" willed (Mark 14:36; compare with Hebrews 5:7; 1 Peter 2:21–25). So Jesus died to bear our punishment, and He rose again to prove that His payment was sufficient. No one will be justified in God's sight because they successfully proved to God that they were better than others. Instead, we must approach Him humbly—like the tax collector who "would not even lift up his eyes to heaven, but beat his breast, saying, 'God, be merciful to me a sinner!'" (Luke 18:9–14).

How does humility grow? Following Jesus requires humility. And growth as a Christian requires growth in humility. Christians grow in humility as we learn to submit to God's inscrutable sovereignty over our trials like Jesus did. God has numerous purposes in every trial that He allows in our lives, yet we are likely aware of only a few (Job 1–2; Psalm 119:71; John 15:1–2; Romans 5:2–5; 8:28–29; 2 Corinthians 1:3–4; 4:16–18; Philippians 3:10; Hebrews 12:5–11; James 1:2–3). And God chooses not to reveal most of the explanations we want (Ecclesiastes 3:11; Deuteronomy 29:29).

What is mature humility? We've now arrived back at the place where Psalm 131 begins. Mature humility is when believers tell God, "[Your reasons are] things too great and too marvelous for me" (v. 1; compare with Job 42:1–6). We're mature when we're like weaned children—calm even though our "tummies are growling" for answers (v. 2). Immaturity—*arrogance!*—is revealed when we insist that God explain Himself to us. So David wasn't bragging when he declared his intention to trust God without knowing His purposes. He was humble! Believer, you can "hope in the Lord," even when you're hungry to know the mysteries of His providence (v. 3). Tell God right now: "I'm not going to be arrogant, God, and insist on explanations. I will trust You, even though I don't understand why You're doing what You're doing in my life."

Let the gospel produce in you a mature humility that mirrors your Savior's. —JOE

True, Kind Love—That Never Ends
READ PSALM 136

DAY 28

*"Give thanks to the L*ORD*, for he is good, for his steadfast love endures forever."* PSALM 136:1

I am a writer by trade and a very picky wordsmith, so, no surprise—I love a good thesaurus. When I see that in *every single verse* of Psalm 136, there is a repeated idea—*God's steadfast love endures forever*—I want to know more. In Hebrew, "steadfast love" is one word—*hesed*. I grew up with a Bible that translated this as "lovingkindness." Other Bible versions fill this concept out for us: It's God's graciousness, loyal love, mercy, compassion, faithful love, steadfast love, kindness. Caution!—Don't oversimplify the beauty of this unique, complex, multifaceted Hebrew word. The synonyms help us grasp the depth of God's care for us. So, what does this uniquely organized psalm tell us about the lovingkindness of God?

God's steadfast love is eternal. The psalm's repeated phrase says that His love lasts eternally. It's a love that endures forever. God's kindness to us is supremely loyal. It will never stop, never fail, never end. It's timeless.

We know that "repetition aids learning." But when I see the exact same words twenty-six times, I can easily think, "Okay, I get it. God loves me. Forever." However, God is the Master-Author—so any redundancy in His writing is intentional. And when someone tells us the same thing over and over again, we believe it more. So, when God says the same thing in every verse, it's because He wants this cemented in our minds—that *He never stops loving us. Ever.*

God's steadfast love is demonstrated in real life. Every verse of Psalm 136 ends with a line that's the same—"For His steadfast love endures forever." But the opening line of each verse varies. Starting in verse 4, the writer chronicles all kinds of situations where we see this faithful love of God to us. And the psalm's opening and closing framework for all these statements is a context of *thanksgiving*. It's a psalm commanding us to give thanks to the good and supreme God for all He has done (vv. 1–3, 26), for all the times, all the ways, all the places where He has been faithful.

- *Give thanks to the God Who made this world (vv. 4–9).* He created this incredible universe—heaven and earth, sky and solar system. He gave us incredibly powerful lights—the sun, our moon, and countless stars.
- *Give thanks to the God Who redeemed and saved His people Israel (vv. 10–22).* He dramatically rescued Israel from Egypt and led them through a desert-wilderness to their promised homeland, eliminating kings one by one.
- *Give thanks to the God Who cares for us (vv. 23–25).* He is kind to us, provides food for us, and deals with our enemies.

Considered in total, this list is amazing! It catalogs twenty-two times when God has demonstrated His love to His children, all pointing us to His greatest act of lovingkindness: "God shows his love for us in that while we were still sinners, Christ died for us" (Romans 5:8)! I get to the end of this psalm and think, *God's kindness continued faithfully throughout Israel's history, and it's not going anywhere. It continues for me, every day. I have experienced God's love in salvation. And it will never, ever end.*

Sadly, even in the face of God's everlasting, steadfast love, we can be tempted to respond with ingratitude. But Psalm 136 urges us to revolt against any discontentedness we might feel and to praise the Lord for all the mercies He has shown to us.

Let the gospel prompt you to thank God today for His steadfast love toward you.—ABBY

DAY 29

Breathtaking Wonder in the Darkness
READ PSALM 139

"Such knowledge is too wonderful for me, too lofty.... Marvelous are Your works.... How precious also are Your thoughts to me, O God! How great is the sum of them!"
PSALM 139:6, 14, 17 NKJV

Has Psalm 139 ever left you in breathtaking wonder? It should. Its God-focused realties are "too wonderful" and "too lofty" to fully grasp; they are marvelous, invaluable, and innumerable (vv. 6, 14, 17). It wasn't until my early twenties that this song brought me to my knees in adoration. Since then, God has used it to comfort me through several seasons of fear.

King David penned this psalm when he was hiding from violent enemies in the "darkness"—perhaps deep in a cave (vv. 11–12; 19–22). David's enemies were God's enemies because they wanted to end the life of the king through whom God had determined to bless the world (1 Chronicles 17). While David was hunted and hiding, he dealt with his fear by singing about the most fundamental attributes of God. It's remarkable to think that in the blackness of a cave, God's child was composing poetry that transformed his understandable fear into breathtaking wonder. If you are currently experiencing a season of dreadful isolation and fearful darkness, consider truths about God until you sing them in wonder.

"Lord, You know everything about me" (vv. 1–6). David did *not* reason in this way: "Lord, You know everything. Therefore, you know me." Rather, he reasoned in this way: "Lord, You know me because you've 'searched me'—You've gone spelunking in the cave of my life. You've watched every move I've ever made, listened to every word I've uttered, and seen each thought that's crossed my mind. You know me because of thorough, personal research." Now, the only way that God's extensive knowledge of you could be anything other than terrifying is if you've had all of your guilt before God washed clean through the blood of His Sacrifice. For those outside of Christ, the fact that nothing they've ever done is hidden from God means that there will be ample evidence for their condemnation (Hebrews 4:13; Revelation 20:11–12). By contrast, those who have been united to Jesus by faith in His blood can stand boldly before God's holy throne with nothing to fear, and they can find grace to help in their time of need (Hebrews 4:14–16). Christian, consider God's personal attention to every detail of your life until it makes your brain hurt (v. 6)—until it makes you praise Him with awe.

"Lord, You're always with me" (vv. 7–12). In seasons of darkness believers often ask, "God, where are You?" In reality, as David explains, there's no chance that someone who belongs to God could ever go anywhere in this universe to escape God's presence. Even if you tried like Jonah did, you couldn't! Instead, you should affirm with absolute certainty that God is with you no matter where you happen to be. He will be with you in the grave. He's certainly with you in the darkness right now.

"Lord, You constructed me according to Your plan" (vv. 13–16). In his isolation, David meditated on the reality that this was not the first time that God had seen him in the darkness. In the "cave" of his mother's womb, when David was hidden from the view of every other human, God "knitted [David] together" according to God's sovereign blueprint for his life (v. 13). Verse 16 stands out in the Bible as one of the most comprehensive declarations of God's personal sovereignty: He has, as it were, a day planner for each of His children, and in that "book" He has planned out in advance every hour of every day—including every trial.

Even in your dark place, such thoughts about God should lead you to exclaim to Him, "How precious are your thoughts about me, O God! They are innumerable!" (v. 17 NLT).

Let the gospel lead you to breathtaking wonder, even in the midst of darkness. —JOE

God Is Great

DAY 30

READ PSALM 145

"Great is the Lord, and greatly to be praised, and his greatness is unsearchable." PSALM 145:3

The shout of the devout Muslims is, "Allahu Akbar!" It's a public, spoken claim that their "god is the greatest." Then, we've got the late, self-congratulatory Muhammad Ali: "I am the greatest." Even in pop culture, we've got G.O.A.T. debates—who is the "greatest of all time?" So, what do we do with Psalm 145—where Jehovah is declared to be great, unfathomably so, and worth everyone's praise—forever (v. 3)? This can't be just another option among the greats. What are evidences that Jehovah is truly *the* great God, *the* greatest being?

Proof 1: God's great works. Israelites would have heard the words "God's mighty acts" (v. 4) and thought of the creation of the world, the exodus from Egypt, water gushing from a rock, years of daily manna + bonus quail, huge wins in multiple battles, and the sun standing still—literally hundreds of years of incredible "awesome deeds" of God (v. 6). For generations, they had rehearsed these top stories from their national history, all performed by the same powerful God—evidence that He is the greatest.

But God's great works are personal. They're for *us*, not just for Israel. He's kind and good to *all* of us (v. 9)—every day. He does truly great things for our benefit, to bless us. He makes life wonderful for us. There are things we don't deserve to see, do, experience, buy, receive, or discover—and He creates those opportunities for us and lands these gifts in our laps (1 Timothy 6:17). And above all other gifts to us—He sent His Son, Jesus, to be our Savior (1 John 4:14)!

Proof 2: God's great love. This one doesn't fit into American greatness paradigms as nicely because we don't laud people for their love. We rank people on their ability to sing, act, teach, lead companies, play sports—but not on their ability to love. But God says, "I love you more than anyone else does. And here's how I've shown you." "The Lord is gracious and merciful, slow to anger and abounding in steadfast love" (v. 8). He provides for us all the time (v. 14). He is the great Giver—delivering us from hell, satisfying our desires (vv. 16, 19), answering our prayers, and even sending food at the right time (v. 15). Elijah's raven DoorDash experience was real. And so is my own story of His provision during a shopping trip at a time when my family was struggling. God had a man I barely knew appear behind me in line at Aldi, and he paid for all my groceries. Only our great God could've done that—because no one else knew my situation that day, not even that acquaintance. God is great enough to love me by meeting my precise needs.

Proof 3: God's great protection. I haven't had many near-death experiences. But I have friends who have been in accidents or natural disasters. And we live in a world where wicked people try to harm others and where evil forces are at work. And then there's sin—the incredible jeopardy we put ourselves in when we wander off God's path. And yet, God keeps watching over us! Have you experienced God's great care for you? His protection? His response as you've cried for help (vv. 19, 20)? Our great God can rescue us from eternal death *and* keep us safe in this life.

The God of the Bible is the greatest. The stack of data this psalm presents is only a starting point! Meditate further on the aspects of God's character and the works He has done and still is doing in your life that show how absolutely great He is. May you grow in your conviction that He is far above any other being. And may your praise—for this great greatness of God—grow more sweet and more sincere.

> "I will extol you, my God and King, and bless your name forever and ever. Every day I will bless you and praise your name forever and ever." (vv. 1–2)

Let the gospel enlarge your view of the greatness of God. —ABBY

DAY 31

Expressions of Praise in the Psalms
READ PSALM 150

"Let everything that has breath praise the LORD." PSALM 150:6

Michael Barrett calls the book of Psalms "a hymnbook and a handbook" (*The Beauty of Holiness: A Guide to Biblical Worship*, page 175). As a hymnbook, it gives us 150 inspired songs which Scripture commands us to sing (Colossians 3:16; Ephesians 5:19). As a handbook, it teaches us how to worship. The kicker is, if we actually *learned to worship from the psalms* rather than from our Christian subculture (churches, conferences, friends, YouTube videos, and so on), our worship might look a lot different.

The psalms command us to praise God (vv. 1–2). Worship is to be a part of everyday life. The mature Christian worships as much on Monday as on Sunday, daily approaching God in Jesus' name. But this psalm specifically addresses corporate worship: "Praise God in his sanctuary" (v. 1). The model of worship that Psalm 150 provides is wholehearted and full-voiced. It is emotive and energetic. The very first word of the psalm is emphatic: *Hallelujah* leaps out of your mouth—more like a shout than a sigh! But our enthusiastic praise shouldn't be void of thought. Rather, our praise is to be a response to God's "mighty deeds" and "excellent greatness" (v. 2).

The psalms tell us how to praise God (vv. 3–6). Having commanded us to "praise" the Lord five times in verses 1–2, the psalmist now riffs on what that praise should look and sound like. The psalm's roster of instruments is a call to worship in a joyful, skillful, multifaceted way. There's no piano or pipe organ listed, but there are brass instruments, woodwinds, strings, and three kinds of percussion. You get the sense that Old Testament worship was glorious, beautiful, and loud. Allen P. Ross writes, "The sum of the matter is that the overall mood of worship should be celebration in community" (*Recalling the Hope of Glory: Biblical Worship from the Garden to the New Creation*, page 441).

The psalms command us to praise God expressively. Psalm 150 is the psalter's last word on worship. It caps an entire book which describes expressive worship:

- *Bowing (Psalm 95:6)* – In both Testaments, the standard word for worship describes abject humility and adoration of God, symbolized by kneeling or lying down flat.
- *Shouting (Psalm 47:1)* – Worship isn't always silent. It was common in the book of Psalms for worship to be unmistakably boisterous.
- *Clapping (Psalm 47:1)* – Many Christians are offended by clapping in church, afraid of its connection to performances. I get that. But clapping also shows enthusiastic agreement, as when people clap during political speeches. In Scripture, clapping was another expression of joy and overt participation in worship.
- *Lifting hands (Psalm 28:2; 34:1–2)* – Raising your hands in prayer wasn't the invention of charismatic Christians. Rather, Scripture commands the lifting of hands (in both Testaments!) as an expression of dependence, helplessness, or joy.
- *Dancing (Psalm 149:3; 150:4)* – Our text, Psalm 150, lists dancing as a legitimate expression of worship. This was a joyful, physical display of delight in God. It was celebratory, not sensual. But it was a far cry from stoicism.

Not every expression needs to be included in public worship. But if we claim to be biblicists whose sole authority regarding faith and practice is the Scriptures, we should consider why our services are so staid in comparison to the descriptions of worship in the psalms. If anything, New Testament believers should be even *more* expressive of wonder and awe since we better understand the glories of Christ's finished work. God deserves our whole-hearted praise!

Let the gospel inspire you to sing with all your might in praise of our God and Savior.—CHRIS

OTHER RESOURCES FROM
WWW.CHURCHWORKSMEDIA.COM

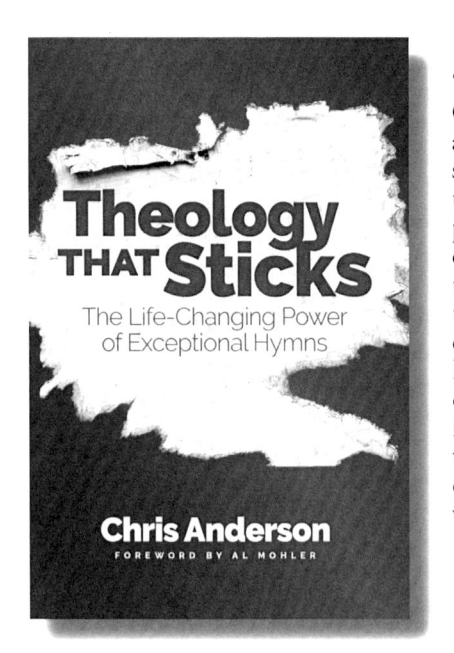

"Christians are a singing people. Our songs both express our devotion and shape us as disciples. Song selection, therefore, is a weighty task. In this warm, accessible, and persuasive book, Chris Anderson offers invaluable guidance on how to choose songs that exalt our triune God, edify His people, and contribute to evangelizing the lost. Packed with a plethora of insightful quotes and loaded with lists of hymns in every category imaginable, this volume is one I wish every pastor, church music leader, and believer would read."

—**Matt Merker**, author, hymn-writer, and Director of Creative Resources and Training for Getty Music

"Here is a book I would love to put into the hands of young adults in my church so that they see that men and women who have left their mark on the mission field were like us in every way, except in their devotion to the God who called them. We need to get rid of our lackluster Christianity in order to fulfill our individual callings, too. This book might be a brief 31-day journey, but M. R. Conrad has packed it with spiritual dynamite. Read it prayerfully. It might change your life—forever!"

—**Conrad Mbewe**, pastor of Kabwata Baptist Church and Founding Chancellor of the African Christian University in Lusaka, Zambia

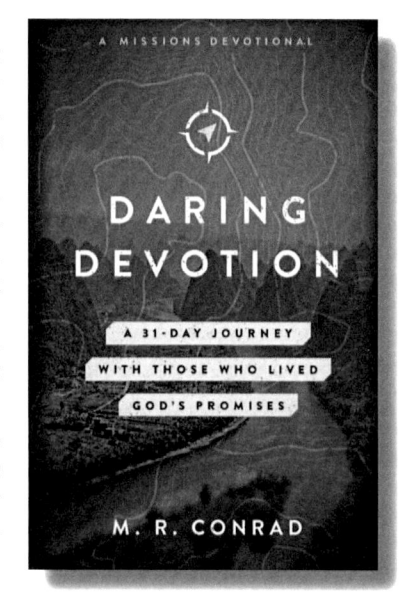

OTHER TITLES IN THIS SERIES

Gospel Meditations for Fathers
"This collection of thirty-one meditations is a must-read for any man striving to fulfill his God-given role as a father. Since each reading is both biblical and practical, it equips the reader to lead family members to greater love to Christ and to God's Word. As parents to four and grandparents to fifteen, Patricia and I recommend this as a fresh resource."
—*John MacArthur*

Gospel Meditations for Mothers
"In the midst of busy days and sleepless nights, moms need the encouragement that only the gospel can give. *Gospel Meditations for Mothers* offers powerful biblical truth and guidance that reminds moms of the importance of their labors and cheers them on in their daily tasks. Whether you're parenting a toddler or a teen, these gospel-focused reflections will minister to your heart as you care for your children."
—*Melissa Kruger*

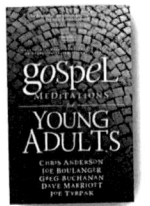

Gospel Meditations for Young Adults
"*Gospel Meditations for Young Adults* is a breath of fresh air for young Christians and for all of us who are raising, discipling, mentoring, or just concerned about them and their spiritual growth and wellbeing. The devotionals are biblical, pastoral, succinct, readable, relevant, and relatable. More importantly, the focus is cross-centered and theological without being forced or trite. This would be a great tool to use in parenting, personal discipleship, group study, or even pastoral counseling."
—*Voddie Baucham*

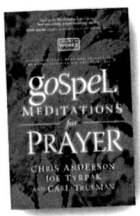

Gospel Meditations for Prayer
"Brief and biblical, these meditations are full of sharp edges. They lead us to pray as cross-bearing disciples of Christ. Yet Anderson, Tyrpak, and Trueman comfort us with Christ's perfect grace for fallen people. So *Gospel Meditations for Prayer* is an encouraging book, but one designed to stretch you."
—*Joel Beeke*

Gospel Meditations for Christmas
"Too often Christmas speeds past us in a blur of busyness and stress, with only the briefest time and the shallowest thoughts given to the Christ that's meant to be at the heart of it all. Give yourself a Christmas to remember by using this profound devotional to pause, ponder, and praise our wonderful Savior."
—*David Murray*

Gospel Meditations on the Reformation
"Theologically rich, thoughtful, and historically rooted devotionals are a rare treat. This volume, which unfolds the theological commitments and pastoral heart of the Reformers, is a unique and enormously helpful devotional."
—*R. Albert Mohler, Jr.*